TAKIRA PAYTON

Advance Praise for

Practice What You Preach

by E.J. "Edge" Bassette

"These ten principles are a must for anyone searching for success. I believe it is impossible to live these principles and fail. All success is not the same. If you are looking for good success and a life of power, then you are ready for these ten principles. This book will help you get it done."

-Zemira Z. Jones

President & General Manager, *ABC Radio Chicago*

"Very insightful reading! E. J. helps us all to raise the bar and step up to a better life and a better future! Must reading for those who want to be challenged to take the next step!"

-Frank C. Bucaro, CSP, CPAE

author of *Taking the High Road: How to Succeed Ethically When Others Bend the Rules*

"Incredible, Inspirational, and Exceptional advice for anyone wanting to achieve more fulfillment at home, in your career, in your life."

-Gregory A. Reid

Sales Vice President and Chief Communications Officer, Yellow Corporation

"E.J. Bassette shares a powerful tool that will change your life. As a corporate manager and a minister, I highly endorse this wonderful work!"

-Nathaniel L. Edmond

Vice President of National Accounts, Reynolds Aluminum Sales Company

"E. J. Bassette is a powerful author because he has proven that you can rise up from your circumstances (read his first, book, *Silent Cry*). In *Practice What You Preach* you will learn how to apply his life principles to your business and your life. Reading this book will prove to be a valuable use of your time."

-Jerry Houston

president of *Houston Associates* and a certified professional behavior and values analyst

"This is a book everybody needs to take on the journey of growth. It will impact you positively, and thereby have an effect on those around you as well."

-Lillian D. Bjorseth

author of *Breakthrough Networking: Building Relationships That Last* and *Nothing Happens until We Communicate* workbook and tape series

"E.J. Bassette's motivational book, *Practice What You Preach,* is a must read for the serious, would-be achiever. It is based on the premise that success should not be left to mere chance. Rather, it should be diligently pursued with an intentional, carefully crafted, systematic plan. Bassette offers a 10-step formula for maximizing one's chances of succeeding in whatever endeavor."

-Rev. Lacy J. Banks

Veteran Baptist preacher, 27-year reporter for the *Chicago Sun-Times* and former U.S. Naval Officer

"This wonderful book gives you a step-by-step formula to improve your life and realize your dreams."

-Brian Tracy

author of *100 Absolutely Unbreakable Laws of Business Success*

"E. J. Bassette takes you deep inside yourself until you find your real self. There he brings you back, helping you to build a path for true success."

-Michael Wynne

author of *The Butterfly Rainbow, The Year of Dreams and Dragons* and *Gold of the Gods*

"This book is an inspirational guide to tapping the greatness that lies within us. Read it and be inspired!"

-Dr. Tony Alessandra

author of *Charisma* and *The Platinum Rule*

"Few books say it better or simpler than this one. *Practice What You Preach* uncomplicates success and puts a life-management system at your fingertips, in a language everyone can understand. I was inspired by E.J.'s insight and wisdom."

-George C. Fraser

author of *Success Runs in Our Race*

"If you practice what E. J. preaches in his book, you'll discover the road to success."

-Jim Meisenheimer

author of *The 12 Best Questions to Ask Customers*

"E. J. Bassette has written a book that will share a bit of his incredible philosophy for life and success. He is a man who consistently makes a difference in people's lives, and this book will make a difference in your life. I recommend that you read it and then re-read it and share it with others. You will be glad you did."

-Willie Jolley

author of *It Only Takes a Minute To Change Your Life* and *A Setback Is a Setup for a Comeback*

"E. J. Bassette is a passionate writer who eloquently addresses essential elements that impact upon whole family education. This book will serve as a change agent for both the young and old."

-Dr. Kimberly Muhammad-Earl
Chicago Public Schools

"Edge Bassette is the ultimate inspirational and motivational author, and *Practice What You Preach* is the apex of his work. Edge has a story to tell, a message to share and lessons guaranteed to help you."

-Vilis Ozals, MBA,CSP
author of *Motivational Leaders* and *GRAND-Stories*

"If you want to connect to the gifts within you, then you will want to read this book. E.J. takes you right to the core... On a wonderful journey that will make it more meaningful and practical to practice what you preach!"

-John G. Blumberg
author of *"Moments of Substance"* C.D.

"A practical roadmap for success and happiness. E. J. "Edge" Bassette's insights are an invaluable tool to help you get to where you want to go. His book is a must read."

-Anthony Galie
author of *Take Control of Your Subconscious Mind*

"This is a must read for anyone who wants to take responsibility for their own success."

-Dr. Frank A. Thomas
author of *What's Love Got to Do With It*

"An excellent book for restructuring one's life and finding self-esteem and self-love. E.J. demonstrates the power in believing in ourselves, accepting our mistakes and learning to move on. He has personally shown how we can never reshape the past, but we can shape the present."

-Dr. Juliet Dinkha, Psy. D.
Diversified Behavioral Services Inc.

4

E.J. "Edge" Bassette   Author of **Silent Cry**

Practice
What
You
Preach

Ten principles for taking

responsibility for your

own success

Powerful Lessons in Change, Procrastination, Failure Recovery and Success

Published by 3B Motivation, Training & Development
P.O. Box 214
Matteson, IL. 60443

Published by
3B Motivation, Training & Development /E.J. Bassette
P.O. Box 214
Matteson, IL. 60443
(708)747-6822
Email: Edge@3Binc.com
Website: www.3Binc.com

Library of Congress Control Number: 2001130932

Library of congress Cataloging-in-Publication Data

Bassette, E.J.
    Practice What You Preach: Ten principles for taking responsibility for your own success/ E.J. Bassette

ISBN: 0-9642800-1-9

   Self Help, Business, Motivation, Life Skills, Success

Jacket Design: Ceata E. Lash
Editors: Peter O' Flaherty & Stuart Hoffman

Printed in the United States of America

Printed by R.R. Donnelly

First Edition: 2001

1 2 3 4 5 6 7 8 9 10

Dedication

To my dear sister, Evette: Although your life was cut short, the legacy of your life will inspire those seeking their dreams, dedication and success. God rest your soul.

To Mom: You joined Evette in heaven just a few months ago. My love for you is unconditional. You have given me the model from God to emulate.

Contents

The circumstances of life/ Learning to get up/ Bad going to worse/ Start now/ What are you worth?/ Change your habits/ Paradigm shifts

Actions speak/ Know where you stand/ Develop your ideas/ A thought with no action/ Productive moments/ Slow down to speed up/ The success plan/ Passion first, plan second/ Create your luck

Know thy self/ Create your environment/ Never too young to learn/ Create lessons for success: Self mastering/A one speech wonder: A speaker is born/ Reality check/ Making a comeback/ Second time around/ A dance with greatness: A lesson from Michael Jordan

The inner journey/ Facts about writing a book/ Time will pass you by: stop blaming/ Grinding it out/ It's not over: forgive and forget/ Look for a brighter day/ Keep pressing forward/ Don't be too busy to count your blessings

Understanding the meaning of success/ Equation for success/ Over "the edge" dream list/ It's never too late to capture your dreams/ Understanding your mission/ What is your life strategy statement?/ Why goals?/ Momma's baby boy, Les Brown: The Motivator/ Everything you want to know is in a book

Foreword

I met E.J. Bassette in 1997. I had heard of the motivational work, he was doing in and around the communities of Chicago a year or so earlier. As a journalist and reporter, I have prided myself in finding out who is doing what in the area of positive change. With all the technology available, in many instances, the best information still comes to me the old-fashioned way, by word of mouth. As information travels about individuals and their works, in the end a person's reputation always seems to precede their good deeds. I know first-hand the importance of building relationships, trust, respect, credibility and longevity for your craft. I have spent my entire career finding out how and why people do what they do.

I've been in the news business for 30 years. I've seen and met the best Chicago has to offer when it comes to individuals making a positive impact and difference. I've also dedicated a large portion of my career reporting on people who use their lives to do extraordinary deeds. I do a news segment on ABC Channel 7 weekday news entitled *Someone You Should Know*. This segment has taken me into every community of Chicago to meet people committed to helping others, while working in the trenches to bring about a change and hope to their fellow human beings.

I have received videotapes and letters from literally hundreds of people seeking to have their good deeds revealed to the public on the *Someone You Should Know* news segment. But it wasn't a videotape, a letter or even E. J. himself who contacted us about an opportunity to be featured. It was that good old-fashioned way, by word of mouth, as my producer saw E.J., first hand doing what he does best, presenting a motivational speech to some Boy Scouts and their parents, including my producer and his son. For the second time, E.J.'s work was brought to my attention. I called him and asked him to do the news segment.

I explained to him that I wanted to videotape him live during a motivational presentation, and asked him for some upcoming dates.

E. J. agreed to participate in the segment if three conditions could be met. He asked if we would video him speaking to young people in a school setting. He explained that he wanted to highlight the youth of America. E. J. also asked if we could show his old neighborhood, the South Side housing development he grew up in and wrote about in his first book. Thirdly, he wanted us to highlight the reasons for his current success: his wife and kids.

That conversation left me with a lasting impression of a young man who was not seeking attention for attention's sake. Instead, he wanted to make people aware of the road he had traveled and of the road they needed to take to make life better for themselves and others. I was impressed that someone from his generation was conscious about his role in effecting change.

Once at the South Side high school, E.J. electrified the teenagers with his words of encouragement. Then he escorted me and my camera crew down to the Ida. B. Wells Housing Project. We videotaped the neighborhood where he was raised and where some of his lifelong friends had fallen prey to the streets. We ended the session by talking extensively about his wonderful wife and kids, how they supported his leaving corporate America to start his motivational company and to write books.

After the session, he asked me as many questions about my life and family as I had asked him. I knew this was a special day and E. J. was a special man. I let him know how proud I was of him and the work he was doing. He really made my job easier.

Since E.J. appeared on *Someone You Should Know* three years ago, he has stayed in touch with me. I believe I met more than a man on a mission; I met a man who practices the principles that he teaches in this book each and every day.

I know by reading this book, you will have a chance to learn those principles he is sharing, tapping into his insight, wisdom and life lessons. When you come into contact with E. J. through his books, tapes, presentations or just a conversation, I believe that, just as I did, you will walk away practicing something new and becoming a better person.

Believe me when I tell you that I've been around the best and E.J. Bassette is definitely *Someone You Should Know*.

Harry Porterfield
Anchor Reporter *ABC 7 News/ WLS Television Chicago*

Preface

So many things have transpired since I had the idea of writing this book. I actually wanted to start this book a year after I completed my first book, *Silent Cry* in 1995. I even anticipated the style and content of this book's motivational self-help style when I added a self-exam at the end of *Silent Cry*. *Silent Cry* tells about the life I lived; this book shares the insight, wisdom and knowledge that got me where I was trying to go. I anticipated this book, but what I didn't anticipate was the amount of change that would take place in my life after 1995. I thought I would finish this book by 1998; here it is 2001.

The changes in the last five years have caused delays, disappointments, setbacks, and even disbelief. But in the end, I had to go to the very principles I wrote about in this book to gain the inner strength to complete this book. I'm the first to admit that this book was written for me, first. I often wondered what life would be like if I had a set of principles that held me to total responsibility for my success, while allowing the best of my potential to shine.

Before writing this book, I asked many people in the hundreds of workshops and speeches I have conducted. "What would your life be like if you had a blueprint for your definition of success that you could follow?" Many of them replied that their lives would be more fulfilling. They would pursue their dreams more vigorously, and their relationships with others would have more meaning.

I challenged myself to write this book so that it would help others, including me, to achieve these goals. To do that, I drew from many sources: the 15 years of notes from seminars and trainings I attended. Hundreds of books and tapes I've read and heard. Corporate experiences, my marriage and experiences from raising my three children. I also drew on stories, insights and wisdom I've gained from conversations with many friendships over the years. And I've relied on common sense and formed many of my own thoughts. So let's take this journey together, and look over the Edge.

Acknowledgements

I must add that none of this would have been possible without the help of these outstanding people. To my wife, Donna: You have been my inspiration. With your love, support, kindness and consistency you have made the first eighteen years of our relationship a joy.

To my three children: Deanna, DeMario and Dominique: You are the joy of my heart, the answer to my prayers and the future of my dreams. Thanks for allowing me to just be dad, which is the best gift in the world to me.

To my dad, Ernest : There is no man who has ever been as great an influence in my life. You are the one who taught me how to be the man and father I am today.

To my seven older sisters and brothers: I have come to value each of your talents and skills. You all have been heroes to me. I've seen each of you share unconditional love for the family. Please know that you are all winners in my book.

To my in-laws, Johnnie Mae and Donald: I don't hear too many people say they love their in-laws, but I can truly say you have made a tremendous difference in my life. I thank you for making me your own son.

To all those family and friends-especially Nile Gossett, Sherri Smith, Karen Zinn, my sister, Eldora and my wife, Donna-who read the manuscript early on when it was virtually unreadable: Your positive input was invaluable in the completion of this book. Thanks to Patricia F. Selph and Dr. Kim Muhammad-Earl who read and gave me constructive criticism. Both of you promised and delivered your feedback.

A sincere thank you to Jerry and Julie Houston. Your suggestions were well taken and made this a better book.

A special thanks goes to Peter O'Flaherty: You took this as your personal mission to see this book edited properly. Thanks for being such a great friend and mentor. I've enjoyed the long hours we've shared, talking about books, life and everything in between. Peter, you have been my eyes to Ireland and its great history.

Also, thanks to Stuart Hoffman: Your editing assistance and content adjustments were invaluable. Thanks to my oldest daughter, Deanna: At sixteen years old, you came through for the old man. Without your typing in the corrections, I would still be typing with two fingers on the manuscript.

Thank you, Ceata E. Lash. It is said in the book industry that the jacket cover is what makes a person initially pick up a book. The jacket cover you have designed is a masterful piece of art. I know with this superb cover, thousands will be drawn to it in order to see what's inside. You and your husband, Garrett have been a blessing in my life since the first day we met. A special thanks to my two assistants, Emily Means-Willis and Justina Giggers.

And, finally to my wife, Donna, again: You have been so great with your assistance in managing my projects, supplying the technical, emotional and friendship support. Can you believe it? We've completed our second book, yours is next. I thank God for you each and every day.

1. Start Where You Are Today

"A journey of a thousand miles starts
with the first step."
-Chinese Proverb-

Practice What You Preach

I was beginning the fifth year of my business, when in the blink of an eye, my world and the way I operated in it changed forever. As a consultant who speaks in the area of professional and personal development, training and an author, I was preaching to audiences the message that even with massive change, we all could ultimately still be in control of our destiny, regardless of the circumstances. I had seen from my own experiences and strongly believed that despite setbacks, people could still choose to put themselves in the driver's seat.

I was born and raised the youngest of nine children in Chicago's Ida B. Wells housing projects. During those formative years, I had seen and was engulfed in the violence and poverty that were harsh realities in some neighborhoods in the inner city. My life became the testament to the power of positive role models and self-motivation. I overcame those incredible odds to have success in college as a student and football player. That success continued as I eventually became an award-winning salesman at two Fortune 500 companies.

The road I traveled was long and hard, but that was the price it took to get ahead. I had learned to take the lemons in my life and make them lemonade. For example, I had taken those experiences of my earlier years and detailed them in my first book, entitled, *Silent Cry*.[1] I had walked away from my corporate job with a major Fortune 500 company, and now I was doing what I believed was my passion, purpose and mission. For the previous four years, I had been reinventing myself and was headed in a new direction, seeing the good, the bad, and the ugly of the speaking and writing industry. I had just entered what I call the *grunt years* of my speaking career, after the initial honeymoon period.

You see, five years ago, I would have imagined myself further along in my business. I would have thought that simply writing a book would automatically make me successful.

---

[1] Autobiography by E. J. Bassette, *"Silent Cry", released in 1995*

But four years later, things weren't exactly as I planned. Everything wasn't happening as quickly as I wanted it to happen. And I wasn't doing everything I needed to do, to make it happen. I was coming to a realization that I didn't have all the answers. I needed to do things differently if I wanted different results. Inside, I didn't know if I was up for that task. I didn't know if I was finally out of my league. But, even when I started doubting myself, the one constant and positive influence was my wife, Donna who still believed in me.

Even when my beliefs started to flounder, a new year brought new goals and expectations for Donna. She had been holding on to one particular goal for a number of years, and that was her desire to move out of our small townhouse into a new home. She reminded me of the promise I had made twelve years earlier. I had promised her back then that we would live in that townhouse for only five years, then move into a house. By then our growing family would need more space. But, like many of you, plans always changed and something always seemed to come up, and I found convenient ways to put it off. The timing was never right.

The other thing that I didn't want to admit was that the last four years had taken a lot out of me. As an entrepreneur, I had given my business all the energy I thought I had and now it just didn't seem like enough. My book had done all right, but it hadn't become a blockbuster, and was not selling as well as I originally expected. Although, I had been doing upwards of one hundred and fifty speaking engagements a year, I rested on my successes instead of developing other markets.   Then suddenly, out of nowhere, my regular business seemed to be disappearing. I was caught between industries and struggling to figure something out. You see, I had left my job and weekly paycheck for the opportunity to make my own path. But that, in itself, was obviously not enough. After four years, I thought the path was supposed to be getting easier, but instead, maybe by my own doing, it seemed to be getting more difficult.

The good news was that my fears weren't fazing Donna. She moved forward with the plan for a new home. She had been watching the Home and Garden Network, and now she was full of ideas, dreams and action. I knew she was on a mission when I noticed that she had started packing boxes and stacking them in the family room. At first, I thought she was packing things to give away to charity until I looked in a box and realized she was packing to move. She calmly explained to me that by packing she was simply claiming that new house. She let the fear of living in that townhouse forever motivate her into action.

We did have one problem: we had no prospects to buy our townhouse. But Donna was determined to pack with or without me. I tried to explain my point of why having a huge mortgage and the constant upkeep on a house would put pressure on me. I wasn't a tool-carrying, fix-it-up type of guy. Second, I explained that a home would take my attention away from all my business and family demands. I kept the excuses coming as I now had this second manuscript I had begun working on, as well as a new business plan I needed to implement. But she said that although I had never considered myself a writer, yet I still wrote a book and was now working on a second one. So even though I had never owned a house, I could learn to become a home owner. But deep down inside, I faced some larger issues. My greatest fear was that if I got too invested, I would have to always produce. And if I couldn't succeed, I would be a failure and the house would be taken away. So I was looking at the glass being half empty instead of half full. I had simply settled for less because less had become comfortable.

But I decided to be open-minded and turn things around. I went with Donna's lead as we put our townhouse on the market, and began our search for a new home. Because of the unique guidelines of the townhouse contract, we couldn't find any buyers. Ideally, we wanted to time the sale of the townhouse and the purchase of the new house as closely as possible to try to keep expenses down. We figured there would be a period of a week or two where we would live with my mother-in-law while in transition.

But, as we found out, the house-buying process became an overrated experience from hell. Not to mention the stress of finding and agreeing on a new community and home to settle into. After searching high and low, we finally settled on a home in a quiet upscale area. So to get rid of the townhouse, we wound up taking a huge loss on the place. Then a problem arose when the new house didn't meet it's market value. To make matters worse, our real estate agent quit her job in the middle of the deal going bad. With no agent, we tried to deal with the sellers directly. The couple we were trying to buy the house from had taken the appraisal personally. They became rude to us and decided not to sign the waiver releasing the $2,000.00 earnest money we had put on the house contract.

We were stuck in a battle with them over a house that we couldn't buy, and a contract they wouldn't let us out of. The contract also prevented us from bidding on other houses. I had heard the horror stories of the real-estate industry and now we were in knee-deep. I had to get a new real estate agent, E. Dwayne Staton, and a lawyer to help get us out of this mess. Now without the townhouse, we all moved in with my mother-in-law for an indefinite period of time, while starting the whole house-hunting nightmare all over again. To make matters worse, while moving our belongings into storage, my business computer crashed, losing four years of clients and data. At a time when I needed the business the most, I lost the ability and resources to keep in touch with my customers. My business almost came to a halt overnight.

Unfortunately, unknown to us, the house-moving fiasco and the computer mess would become the least of our problems. In the midst of my own stress and chaos, I received a call saying the youngest of my six sisters, Evette, had been admitted into the hospital with flu-like symptoms. Within the week, those symptoms worsened, leaving her with a life-threatening illness.

I, along with my parents and seven sisters and brothers, was caught off guard and couldn't believe that this untimely nightmare could be happening to her. At the age of thirty-nine, she had just taken control of her life by leaving a bad marriage, graduating from college, getting a new job, and moving her three teen-age children out of a crime-ridden community into a home of her own. In a little over a year, she had made all these changes as her nursing career had taken off to a great start.

I tried to put my business and house problems on the back burner in order to devote time to Evette and her illness. My other five sisters are especially to be commended for the love, energy, sacrifice and time they showed toward Evette. Dad was there on the spot to see after his youngest daughter and Mom prayed for God to show his love and mercy on her. We all pitched in to help her and her children.

Donna was trying to keep me sane because she knew I wasn't handling all this very well. I was dealing with Evette, the house, the business, and our own three children. We wanted them to stay focused on school and activities during this difficult time. I tried to take it a day at a time, while trying to make sense out of a senseless situation. We continued to look for a house as we all did our best to try to keep Evette positive.

In the midst of all these situations, when I thought things couldn't get any worse, yet still another unbelievable incident occurred in my life. While I was taking my eight-year-old daughter to school, the police pulled me over, humiliated me, then arrested and handcuffed me. To make matters worse they, locked me up in jail. I was being falsely accused, framed, lied about and treated like a common criminal. Things were happening so fast, I couldn't control my life as it spiraled out of control.

Here I was, a husband, role model, community leader, author and professional speaker. I had been spending my life teaching and helping others to develop their character to overcome their obstacles, and now I was the one needing all the help. After growing up in the projects and escaping the violence, I had heard that one never really escaped the stigma of their past. Which was I going to believe? I had never been locked up or in handcuffs my entire life. Now at thirty eight-years old, this is what my reality had become. Every minute seemed like a lifetime because I wasn't prepared for the madness that was in my life. As I sat in jail, I closed my eyes and thought about the courage Evette had to have to overcome the prison of her illness. I thought about all the people that had been subjected to greater injustices than me. I had to face the reality that I wasn't above the lies and deceits that others bring into one's life. I just hadn't ever felt the sting of a situation like this until I was the one in it. I now realized I wasn't above it.

Over the previous four years, I had lectured over 600 times in front of hundreds of thousands of people. Now within a few months, my entire life was being turned inside out. I was literally walking around in shock. I couldn't believe someone could simply make up a lie and my only recourse would be to go through the initial punishment and abuse, then defend myself in court. I was forced to get an excellent lawyer to defend me. I spent the time and money to go through the court system to clear my name, reputation and gain my innocence. But by the time I was put through the entire experience, I was left with mental paranoia about how far people would go to destroy me or my family. I suddenly lost that ability to trust, smile and care for others that had become a trademark for my success over the years. My speeches and seminars suddenly took on a different dimension as my clients noticed a change in my behavior. I didn't want to interact with my audiences, as I became distant and aloof. Many of my nights were even worse because I was full of aggravation and fear, as I sat up wondering-would someone else come after me?

Internally, I constantly struggled with the embarrassment and guilt of my problems. I also regretted the valuable time I spent dealing with my own problems, and how they were keeping me so occupied that I didn't have the time to resolve or deal with Evette's problems effectively. All these events had piled on top of each other, and the weight of the burden made me live in absolute fear of what could happen. I abandoned everything I knew and was starting to cower under all the pressures I was experiencing. We were still living at my mother-in-law's when I won my court case, but Evette's condition continued to worsen. She was overcome by her illness and died in October of 1999. I was devastated, along with others in the family, as we were left to pick up the emotional and psychological pieces.

I personally had to make some tough decisions on what I was going to do about my future. I had business coming in that was already on the calendar. But new business had completely dried up; the phones had stopped ringing. I would have to be insane to continue when I had so much stacked against me. Maybe, I didn't have what it takes to make it in this business. I didn't want or need to go through all the work it took to write another book. I had spent many years and much money working on my first book. I knew it had made an impact on those who read it. But it was a long and hard process for just so few rewards. Maybe all this motivation stuff was just a bunch of lofty ideas. Why was I going to try so hard when others simply took my life efforts and reduced them to a one-sentence sound bite?

After all, I had been through so much that I didn't know if I had enough in me to push forward. So I talked with Donna, after deciding to give up the speaking business and just get a job. Donna responded by confiding her belief in me as she re-shared our dreams together. She helped me see through some of my pain and fears. After we moved and settled in our new house, she started putting my computer back together. I started reading through this manuscript, which was in the very early stages. I became empowered by reading my own words. I knew a large part of my future success hinged on my following my own advice. I read what I had written about Evette before she made her transition. It made me remember how proud I was of her and of what she had accomplished. I had constantly shared with her my joy for what she had done. I felt the energy and excitement I had once shared before all these events happened. I knew I had to pick which road I wanted to travel, the one up or the one down. Would I give up and give in?

Did I really come this far to leave my dreams behind? Would I let my *faith and experiences* kick in and go on to *practice what I had preached* to my self and others all my life? Could I walk on that faith and know that all my life experiences could be used as hope for others in their time of need? Could I remember the good Evette and others shared in my life? I decided to pick up this manuscript again as it sat dormant in the computer and make it the inspiration and guideline I needed. I decided to finish it, rebuild my career and take it to the highest level possible. As I stated before, I had to go back and follow my own advice, which is the toughest thing to do. I fell back in love with life. Did that mean that I would never have any other problems or worries? No, but it would give me better reference points to handle the situations as they came up.

I totally changed directions in my business. I started seeking out better *centers of influence*. In order to succeed, I decided to go to a higher level. I reevaluated my life and decided to find new mentors, business opportunities and relationships. I started working on this manuscript with the same passion I had with *Silent Cry*. I started offering new services with my training and developed an affiliation with a wonderful training company called Houston Associates. My company, 3B Motivation, Training & Development developed a win-win relationship with Jerry and Julie Houston, the founders of Houston Associates.

Within a year, I started to get things back running smoothly. Then another family tragedy came to our door. This time it was our family's first lady and spiritual leader, my mom. Momma went home to be with the Lord on September 2, 2000. She had taught me to pray and to believe and trust God with all my heart. Momma asked us all to praise God when she left this Earth, because that simply meant she would be with her Lord and Savior.

Because over the previous year, I had put myself in a better place to practice what I preach, I was in a better place to react positively to my mom's wishes. I love you, Mom, and I know that you and Evette met at the gate of heaven to rejoice with your sister, Florence, your brother, Buddy and your mom, and all the others that have gone on before us.

I know as long as I walk this earth, by living my best life, I can truly make a difference. Now, I want to challenge you to read this book, to put into practice the things you preach in order to live your best life.

The circumstances of life

You have to make the same commitment to move on with your life. If you could fast-forward your life to the very end, by examining your life in retrospect, you would see there were several major *circumstances* that possibly shaped the course of your entire life. Those circumstances caused you to make the decisions or indecisions that sent you down the paths you took in your lifetime. In other words, those major circumstances led to certain consequences. I call those major *circumstances* the *defining moments* that took place in your life. When looking back, you'll realize that those defining moments were the difference between whether you soared to greatness or staggered in mediocrity.

Now take a moment and think of the magnitude of what a few majors decisions can have on your entire life. You may ask yourself, how can I be in control of my circumstances when things just seem to happen? Remember, just like I learned, you can't control what happens to you, but you can control how you handle it.

Everybody is born with certain gifts and talents. The "X" factor becomes what expectations to add to those attributes. There really is a thin line between where we are and where we want to be. The difference becomes your ability to do that little extra to change your circumstances and alter destiny in your favor.

Think about your life today. You may realize you are not that far away from what you want, need and desire. Your life's destiny is hanging on those few decisions you know you need to make. Those decisions will automatically cause you to make choices, while also forcing you to do things differently. Picture your life as being one of the teams in a championship game. As in life, two teams usually come into the game evenly matched. Usually, the difference between the eventual winner and the other team is a subtle bounce of the ball, a missed play, a mental mistake, or a few bad choices. At the end of the game when a champion emerges, the other team knows they had a chance, but in the end, only one held on to win.

In the winner's locker room, you see celebration and exuberance. The players talk about how they wanted it a little more, executed the right judgment at the right time and played the game and made good decisions with their defining moments, where it counted most. They walked the walk and talked the talk.

The other team talks about the mistakes they made and how they let the game slip out of their hands. They also talk of next time. Unfortunately, many teams and players never get another chance. The team gets old, injuries set in and players get traded. Which team do you want to be on? The team that puts together the right plays and executes them, or the team that wishes for a second chance?

I believe you picked up this book because you wanted to be the winner you already know you are, within. You just have to come to the game of life prepared to play the game on the field. You need to have one of those defining moments and life-changing circumstances happen in your favor.

27

You see, everyone has dreams of doing great things, touching someone's life in a positive way, or making an emphatic and undeniable impact on the world. We want others to view us as trustworthy and dependable, and seek our encouragement, advice and support. We seek loyalty, while asking others to respect and validate the value of our words and deeds. And most of all, we desire to be understood, to have love, passion and adoration in our lifetime, while being fulfilled with happiness and success.

Did you know that your life has the capacity to evolve into all those things and much more? You may ask, why don't these good things happen for everyone? That's because many let the excuses become a factor, for example, "I got what it takes, but I'm not ready yet." You could apply your resources in a way that could have you soar in all your chosen fields of endeavor. But you have to be ready when the opportunity comes by tapping into the necessary ingredients to get the desired results.

A man once said, "It is a funny thing about life. If you refuse to accept anything but the best, you very often get it." On the other hand, by not being ready for the best, you can leave your *resources* dormant and take an easier way out, by blaming, pointing fingers and lacking discipline and direction. Don't give in to complaining about long hours, little compensation and even less recognition. Don't let lost loves and even fewer true friendships become the reality of your life.

Many people often find themselves vacillating between different attitudes trying to practice what they preach. You can find your own words becoming less valuable, creating a vacuum between what is and what should be. Remember, no one can motivate you. The responsibility of your life journey falls squarely on your own shoulders. Others can simply point you in the direction or the road leading to where you ultimately want to go.

What road to success do you choose to travel? Is it winning the race, gaining the grand prize, being the hero or having the love and admiration you deserve? You can access your *resource of dreams* by searching your subconscious mind. Knowing the list of dreams exists is critical to understanding how you approach your day using the effort and time on things that are important. (All of these topics will be discussed in detail.)

How do you choose? It is said that the dreams we seek most as adults are those things we were deprived of as children. So think back to when you were younger and try to recall your childhood dreams. What did you want to become? Why were those things so important to you then? Why did you stop pursuing those dreams?

In my motivational development training with small children (kindergarten through fourth grade), I've had many candid conversations about their ambitions and dreams. These young people dream of becoming doctors, lawyers, teachers and world figures, creating life-saving inventions, becoming rich and famous or just being a force in everything possible.

As I think back, one particular first-grader comes to mind. He wanted to become all those things I listed above in one lifetime. Even more incredible than his dreams, was the fact that he lived in one of the poorest housing developments in Chicago, a place where most adults had abandoned their own dreams.

This boy, like most children, was not inhibited by background, gender, economic class or race. They seem to overcome the doubts and fears that most adults share. Children use many of the *practice what you preach* principles naturally. Allowing them the ability to think past fear of failure expands their level of thinking well beyond their years in age.

Did you know you were born not knowing fear of failure? Fear is passed down as a learned behavior. When I've shared my findings about children and their outlook with my personal and professional development workshop participants, some adults have gotten defensive, saying things like, "Children just don't know any better," or "They haven't been hit with the realities of the real world yet." Unfortunately, it's many adults who have let life's challenges inhibit them. Obstacles like reality, time constraints or lack of family support have stopped them from believing in themselves and their dreams. This sends most adults into what I call a *dreamless stage*. This stage allows complacency and procrastination to set in, with a mental death not far behind. Someone once said, "Where there are no dreams, the only things left are nightmares." I'd like to offer you a different way of thinking. The way of an open mind, and, better yet, a solid life plan and tools to follow.

In learning the principles to practicing what you preach, you'll be encouraged to remember the hard knocks of your past experiences, along with the limitations they have placed on your future outlook. But that's all you'll do with the past, is learn and remember. You will also remember the joys of being an ageless child, when things were simple and carefree. You'll be encouraged to dig deep into those memories to find the dreams you've buried, but once had. You have to know where you've been to see where you're going. The principles will reinforce the old adage, "Learn from your past, live for today and plan for tomorrow."

I'd like to associate the principles of *practicing what you preach* with babies learning to walk for the first time. They'll reach their hand out to hold onto an object, while trying to take a step. Even after they fall, they'll try again and again, until they get it right. Sometimes they fall on their faces and they'll even cry. But they'll always find the courage and confidence to stand up again. Learning from the first fall helps them do it better the second time. In other words, they adjusted the plan from those earlier failures or falls and now they're having successes. The same can be true for you. Once you fall, get up and try again while learning and growing.

Preach Points:
- Your toughest critic is yourself
- Don't lose the child inside of yourself
- Always be open for change

Learning to get up

Remember, like a baby, you're learning from each fall after your attempted step. Whether the step is good or bad, you want to grow and learn from the experience. This lesson of growth hits close to home in my own life. I learned a valuable lesson from my oldest brother, Eddie. When I was a teenager, he came to me with a dream of starting a family business. Eddie, the second oldest in a line of nine siblings, is seventeen years older than I am. He has always been the family dreamer and the one, we all figured would strike it big.

Eddie's dream started back in the Ida B. Wells housing projects of Chicago in the early 1960's. He decided to go to college at a time when most young African-American men never seriously looked at college as an option. While others settled for working factory jobs, Eddie focused in on what he thought he did better than anything else. Since he was a small boy hustling newspapers, he valued money. So, accounting was the business he desired. Eddie enrolled in college, seeking a four-year degree in accounting. Eddie struggled, while constantly being discouraged by many of his professors. They repeatedly told him the Black community would not and could not support Black professionals, like lawyers and accountants. Because of this discouragement, and lack of academic support, he found his path long and difficult. But Eddie's self-discipline kept him practicing what he believed until he reached his goal of becoming the family's first college graduate and accountant.

Eddie always prided himself as an African-American man who valued and respected the progress made during the Civil Rights movement of the 1960's. Eddie also wanted to take full advantage of the new choices he was now able to make. With hard work and determination, he found the corporate door opened, allowing him the opportunity to achieve success in corporate America as the comptroller of a major hospital.

Bad...going to worse

However, by the late seventies, Eddie's dream of the brass ring was interrupted by a crash into an unforeseen "glass ceiling." He faced racism and other obstacles that finally prevented him from further promotional opportunities. Eddie reevaluated his plans and decided to leave the corporate structure to start his own business.

Now Eddie had to stop and decide what was his passion. Then he had to incorporate that passion into his life skills. (Passion will be discussed later.) Eddie had decided on what business he could do best, and the answer to that question led him into the carpet business. After a few years, the business began to make major strides. Eddie's long-term business plans included my working alongside him, making it a true family operation. Unfortunately, before I could graduate from college, he and the business hit an unimaginable streak of bad fortune.

Before we continue with Eddie's story, stop and ask yourself the following question. Don't read on until you answer it.

What do you do best ? _____.

Preach Points:
- Focus on what you do best
- Take full advantage of the choices
- Constantly reevaluate your plans

In times of good health and spirit, you must continue to develop skills by working on your weakest areas. I like to call them *personal steps*-the things that allow you to grow from within. I contend that if you are not unleashing all of your abilities, then you're not giving yourself a full chance for success, and that leaves you vulnerable for your upcoming situations.

We all have natural gifts and abilities to excel in life. We all have the genius within us-physically, mentally, emotionally, financially and spiritually-to do what we want. But when we don't follow our lessons learned, or practice listening to that *inner subconscious voice*, we stand still, thus losing ground on our prescription for success. We ignore what is called *subconscious belief* or an *intuitive feeling*. This causes us to lose our natural abilities to reason, lessening our blessings as we become physically, emotionally, mentally, financially and spiritually crippled.

Eddie always preached brotherhood and the sharing with his fellow man. But there were a few subconscious beliefs that he knew to follow before he heeded to those rules. First, he knew that everybody who looks like you is not your brother in action, heart and spirit. And secondly, he knew that when you conduct business, you have to always look into someone's work history and see if there are any red flags. Eddie knew and preached these principles to me, but made exceptions in his own decisions. Eddie ignored his subconscious beliefs and his kind spirit got in the way of his business sense. He gave a friend total access to his growing business and product line. Eddie believed his own honesty was valid enough to make his friend a partner. This logic backfired within a short period. His new partner began stealing carpet inventory, sending the business into deep debt, and eventual bankruptcy.

During the same period, Eddie's personal life took a turn for the worse when his wife of fifteen years filed for divorce, and began the process that eventually took the house, kids and the car. Everything Eddie worked for was gone. He was now in his late thirties, financially at rock bottom and practically homeless. Running out of options, he moved back into the projects with Dad. With his last savings, he purchased an old model car to get around in-and I do mean old. His car was so rusted out that when he stopped at red lights, he would pick up rusted parts off the street and patch them back on the car before he started on his way.

Start now

On my first visit home from college, I saw Eddie. He looked drained and beat up by the world. Things worsened when Dad and Eddie parted ways as roommates, leaving him desperate to find another place to stay. Eddie paused for a moment to catch his breath. He knew he couldn't live in the past; he had to learn from his mistakes. So he put a plan together and started from that day to live in the *precious present,* one day at a time.

First, he moved in with a family friend who loved and believed in him. Next, he started using his accounting skills to make a modest living. Finally, he looked for people who would be supportive of his efforts, including me. So every time I came home from college to visit, Eddie seemed to know I was in town. He would call me early in the morning, sometimes as early as 6 a.m., asking me to drive over to give his car a jump-start. Though he was down financially, what amazed me most was that his spirits were always high. His outlook on life and his future was even higher because he had a plan. As I completed my last year of college, Eddie shared his ultimate plan with me. Eddie's plan was for us to work together. In Eddie's words, I would be the "combination to the lock" that he had been looking for to get fully back on his feet.

After college I moved back in with Dad and gave Eddie the green light, agreeing that we would work together. Dad, on the other hand, had come from a different school of thought-the old school. Dad was from Mississippi, the land of conservative thinking that stressed, "Get a good job and keep it forever." I had heard all of Dad's old war stories of how he walked ten miles to school and had never missed a day of work in thirty years. In other words, Dad wasn't too happy with the idea of my not looking for what he called "a real job." He was even more upset when he found out that my weekly wages were averaging only about fifty dollars.

Eddie made me a salesman, and even though that included no formal training, he did share the keys of being professional in my outlook and attitude. Although I learned a lot, I must admit, as time moved on, the car I owned quickly began to fall apart. Dad's patience for our business venture began to wear thin. Dad went along with the idea for the first year, but during year two, he said that if I didn't get a real job, I had to move out of the spacious South Side lake-front property known as the Ida B. Wells housing projects. I wondered, where do you go when you're getting thrown out of the projects?

I knew I had to make a move, so I asked my college sweetheart, Donna, whom I loved dearly, to marry me. Donna had just gotten her first job after college, making just over $15,000 a year. She didn't think marriage was the best idea because of my financial situation. I finally convinced her that marrying me was the right move.[2] We took the salary she made and put it with the fifty dollars a week I made. We budgeted as a family, not letting money be the factor of dictating our attitude or love for each other. While jumping into a new life together with both feet, we planned and were able live below our financial means.

Within that next year, I wanted to take on the world, but with a wife and now, a new baby. Donna started to worry about some of the things that would provide for a more secure future. That meant becoming better off financially. I was caught

---

[2] See *Silent Cry,* part IV by E.J. Bassette

between the dreams of my brother's business and the obligations I had to my wife and daughter.

Preach Points:
- We all have gifts
- Always keep your spirits high
- Don't get thrown out of the projects

"If you place little value on yourself, rest assured the world will not raise the price."
-unknown-

What are you worth?

I had to make a decision on how I was going to handle Eddie, the business and my family responsibilities. Stress and anger started to surface when both mine and Donna's cars started to have problems. One evening, standing on a Chicago highway alongside my wife's stranded car, all I could think about was the conversation I needed to have with Eddie about how bad things had gotten financially for my family.

When we met the next morning, I was ready to let him have it. But he calmly turned the conversation back in my direction, and asked me a question I'll never forget. He said, "If you are unhappy with the money you're making, name a salary you think you are worth." Caught off guard, upset and frustrated, I shouted out "I'm worth fifty dollars a week!" Eddie immediately explained that I was wrong, and said that if I looked at where I was and went out and worked with the same attitude, character and integrity of a person making $50,000 a year, then that would be the salary I was worth. He explained to me that I had to believe it, then receive it.

That day, Eddie instilled in me the belief that said I was worth much more than I imagined. He said if I worked hard and treated people well, the money would follow and be the last concern I would have in life. As someone said, "In order to do what you've never done, you've got to become someone you've never been." I first had to become someone new from the inside. I left that conversation understanding the principle which Eddie preached, and within in six months, I started working for a major Fortune 500 company, and became one of their sales superstars, making upwards of $50,000 a year.[3] My success didn't start the day I started my new job. I brought the attitude of success with me. Eddie helped me see it and I had to believe it existed.

During my first year in corporate America I had to work to get my sales knowledge and skills to the level of my determination and desire. During that year, I took Eddie's principle and mindfully empowered myself to upgrade my old belief system. I was now practicing the worth principle in full effect. Eddie taught me some valuable lessons that I'm now sharing with you.

That first lesson was to stop and gather myself-not to let my emotions slide me down a slippery slope where I couldn't recover. Then I started from where I was, using that foundation to make things work. Then I improved on what I knew, updating my skill level. Now, you may be at the same point in your life. I want you to stop and think of where you are and where you want to be. Do you want something more? Then first embrace what you already have. Take a moment and write down what is your true worth.

Preach Points:
- Claim your true value
- See it, believe it, achieve it
- Your success is already here

---

[3] See *Silent Cry,* part IV by E.J. Bassette

Change your habits

Now getting to the point of making $50,000 year wasn't a cakewalk. Several negative habits threatened to stop me along the way, and will threaten you also. Remember we are creators of good habits and bad habits. One of the potentially bad ones is the habit of *procrastination*. Procrastination will lead you back to what you're familiar with, regardless of whether it's right or wrong. Most people can't objectively see their own faults. Sometimes you're too close and emotional about your own circumstances. The closeness can allow procrastination to handicap you from applying a full effort into your own self-improvement. Remember, you are not a water faucet, just turning your habits off and on. You'll have to consciously work extra hard to change. Ask someone in your family or a close friend to suggest some areas of improvement. It will be up to you to make the changes they suggest and use self-discipline to make them work from within.

Don't try to change more than one thing at once. That will only frustrate you, leaving a bad taste in your mouth about your overall goal. Remember, it will take at least thirty days of consistently doing one habit differently to bring about the change. Your habits will continue to change as your purpose changes. During this process, stay positive in thoughts and actions. Utilize positive daily affirmations to keep yourself inspired and focused. By staying positive, you will bring positive results, and negative thoughts and actions will bring negative results.

Also remember to be totally aware of keeping this process focused on you and what you can do to change. Accept that you are not very good at the thing you are trying to change. Be aware at home and work of the emotional tension change can bring. Don't attack those who have brought the advice of change to you. For example, the change might be forced on you through a new project, job description or added responsibility. Keep the stress down by being flexible and proactive.

Habits I need to change:

1._____.
2._____.
3._____.

Practice Points:
- Your greatest enemy is procrastination
- Allow thirty days for change
- Ask family and friends for help
- Be flexible

Paradigm shifts

Knowing that you must change helps you to rethink your paradigms. A *paradigm* is the way you picture the world. That picture is reality as you know it-as clear or cloudy as it may be. It is the way you see the world or situation you're dealing with. Henry Ford said it like this, " Whether you think you can or think you can't – you are right." To create a better outlook on a situation, you have to have a paradigm shift or change in consciousness. A change in consciousness allows you to see things differently than before, because your entire outlook has changed. For example, as stated earlier, I had to have a paradigm shift in order to see my true value and worth. My first paradigm had me limiting my earnings to only fifty dollars a week. I had to change my mental state in several areas in order to change that paradigm.

First, was the attitude I had of my worth. I had to decide there was something I could change to make it better. I had to accept the fact I was in my situation because I never developed a desire to change. Second, was the value I placed on my skills. I had to understand a top Fortune 500 company would train me in the sales processes and methods they wanted me to convey with my customers.

Now, you have mental consciousness to make a paradigm shift. You have to start where you are and create a vision. Then begin to focus on the way you want things to be. Remember, certain beliefs cause certain behavior, so know what behaviors in your vision that need to change. Is it your vision that affects your job, lifestyle or financial situation?

You have to discover what you are most *passionate* about, then make your change in that area. A famous quote says, "It is not lack of money or education, but a lack of belief that stops you and me from achieving." Once that paradigm is changed, it forces a different set of events to take place in your life. My shift in consciousness even forced my brother Eddie to rethink the way he wanted to manage his business in the future. "In some ways," he admitted later, "we had become each other's crutch." Having me around caused him to become more complacent than he wanted to be in his business. When it was all said and done, we both had to make paradigm shifts in order to grow and reach the next level. Remember, that first growth was internal and between the ears. Think about some areas where you need to have a paradigm shift and list them.

I need to shift in these areas:

1._____.
2._____.
3._____.

Practice Points:
- Develop a desire to change
- Make things better
- Beliefs cause behavior

2. Develop your Philosophy & Ideas

"The quality of a person's life is in direct
proportion to their commitment to excellence,
regardless of their chosen field of endeavor."
-Vincent T. Lombardi -

Practice What You Preach

Actions Speak

Part of what makes your beliefs hold water is your *true conviction* toward those principles in which you believe. That conviction comes from understanding your *intrinsic values* or *philosophies*. Your intrinsic *values* are the things others can't see, but they can judge through your actions. Those actions are constantly displayed through the essence of what is called your belief system. Life's true value comes when you understand your purpose. Your intrinsic values are manifested through honesty, integrity and your ability to be truthful to yourself and others. What makes your intrinsic values so pertinent is the fact that your total being is dependent on its competency.

Your intrinsic values can be defined in words by having a life's philosophy. The formal definition of philosophy, according to Webster's dictionary, is, "The study of morals and character; study of principles underlying all knowledge; insight applied to life." Philosophies are important because you are headed in a certain direction based on them, whether you like it or not. There is a saying, "The same wind blows on all of us; it's the way we set the sail that makes a difference." That difference is the belief system we bring along with us.

For example, with all the money being paid to high-priced talented athletes, you constantly hear coaches say the players they would rather have are the ones who share the intangibles in the locker room or clubhouse. Those players bring a certain belief, brought on by a philosophy that reinforces a positive attitude and good team chemistry. That chemistry will breed an atmosphere of success, and that is more valuable than talent alone.

The same is true for an employee on your company's team. He or she is bringing their intrinsic values or philosophy to work all the time. You see it first-hand by their work habits, beliefs and how they conduct themselves. It's not what you do, but how you do it. Some people bring an incompetent set of beliefs and operate out of chaos and confusion.

42

Once you are cognizant of practicing your own philosophy, your life will be transformed. You already have a code in you, taught to you by your parents, guardians or other loved ones. You and I live by that code each and every day. It could have been shared with you as a motivational quote, Bible verse or poem.

You remember that as a child, your parents taught you right from wrong. That same code tells you to help others, not to cheat or lie, and to stand for what you believe. It also teaches you not to operate in fear or not to be controlled by that which you fear. Your life's philosophy is reflected in the time, talent and money you spend carrying out your deeds and beliefs. Therefore the saying "Put your money and time where your mouth is" is appropriate for anyone with a true philosophy.

Understand that the depth of your philosophy is directly related to the depth of your beliefs and eventual success. With strong beliefs, you will arm yourself to become unstoppable. By contrast, going against your philosophy, or going against the very things you believe in is a recipe for failure. I want you to take a moment and write down your philosophy. Keep it visible for inspiration.

My life philosophy is_____

_____.

Practice Points:
- True value comes when you understand your purpose
- Everyone has a philosophy
- A strong philosophy will reflect strong values

<u>Know where you stand</u>

As I grow older, my exposure to different people and places has played a greater role in expanding my original philosophy. As we discussed earlier, your *life's philosophy* was probably formed at an early age from a number of *different influences*, like family, friends and environment. I enjoyed corporate America and the field of sales. But I didn't enjoy the corporate games some managers seemed so willing to play. I also saw myself struggling between my newly perceived material success and the lack of commitment to help those people back in my formerly poverty-stricken community. I had come a long way in life and felt indebted to my community. I also knew I wasn't putting back into it what I had received.

As I searched for answers, one gentleman I met in the corporate world taught me a valuable lesson in handling my concern. He described it as the *three ways to share* your available resources. The first way is through your money. If you don't have that, then share your talent. Then, finally, share your time. I knew I wasn't truly giving back in any of these areas.

I believe there is a point in everyone's life when they see time passing by and they wonder if they are a giver. Stop right now and answer that question. Are you a giver who has given back in life what life has given you? Or have you cheated life by holding back, giving in or not doing all you could. I know personally in my heart that I'd been cheating. A recent movie called people like that "takers," people who take everything and give nothing or very little back.

A valuable lesson about being a giver was driven into my heart and mind more strongly than ever a few years ago. I learned that life wasn't about how long you live, but about the impact your values and philosophies have on others. Some people are able to impact humanity, even though their lives are cut drastically short. By standing on their values and philosophies, they are forever remembered for their ultimate sacrifice. Here is a story of how this lesson became crystal clear to me. While I was watching the news one night, a chilling story came flashing across the television screen. Instant horror came to mind once the details of this particular story began to unfold. The story was about a little five-year-old boy, Eric, who had been thrown out of a fourteenth-floor window of an abandoned apartment in a Chicago housing project. This particular housing project had become notorious for poverty, violence and destruction. As I sat there watching this news report, the information started to bring a chilling and numbing effect to my senses.

Two boys, ten and eleven years old, wanted Eric to steal candy from a neighborhood store. Although only five-years old, Eric refused; his mother had already instilled in him a philosophy of not to steal. So, out of disapproval in of the values and philosophies Eric displayed, in a rage, the two older boys took him to one of the many abandoned apartments on the fourteenth floor.

Eric's older brother, who was eight-years old, did all he could to keep his little brother from going into the abandoned apartment. Eric's older brother struggled with the two older boys, but they overpowered him and beat him up. They made Eric get on the window ledge and pushed him out-fourteen floors to the ground. With his little body crushed by the force of the fall, he still managed to hang on to life for two days before he died.

Like most Americans, I was in shock after hearing the details of this tragedy. My own son, who was seven years old at the time, was playing nearby when the news flash caught his eye. My son asked me a question that I'll never forget for the rest of my life. With his eyes fixed on the television, he said, "Daddy, why didn't you save that little boy's life?" You see, I'm my son's hero, and he looks at me as the one man who can do anything. In his eyes, I'm the biggest and strongest man in the world. My son knew I would never let anyone hurt him. So he wanted to know why his dad would let someone hurt this little boy, who looked just like him. I sat there with tears welling up in my eyes because I knew he was right. Maybe I could have donated more time in my old neighborhood. Maybe I could have been a *giver,* having a positive influence on those two boys.

You see, my son didn't know I lived the first twenty-two years of my life in that same neighborhood, watching the community deteriorate. I had known many friends who had succumbed to violence in that same community.[4] So finally I had to ask myself-was I using my talent to do more?

I went back to the neighborhood to attend Eric's funeral. By this time, his life's story had made national headline news. With national attention being focused on the violence among the nation's youth, top political and civic leaders such as Reverend Jessie Jackson and Mayor Daley came with others from across the nation to pay their respects. Hundreds of people who lived in the community also attended.

Feeling helpless, I walked around to view Eric's body as someone placed a teddy bear in his arms. He was just a baby, only five years old. He died doing what he believed was right. By not stealing the candy, his philosophy and value system was set, and out of this tragedy I will remember his legacy.

Do we think this little boy or thousands of others wouldn't have wanted to live a full and productive life? The answer is surely yes. But I knew what Eric had done in five years of life, most of us would never have the courage to do. That is to simply stand on the values and philosophies we believe in, even if it cost us our life. I want you to think about your own value system and philosophy.

Preach Points:
- Share your time, money, talents and time
- Become a giver, not a taker
- Impact other lives with your values and philosophy

---

[4] To read more about Ida B. Wells projects and formative years, read "Silent Cry", part I.

"There is one thing stronger than all the armies in the world, and that is an Idea whose time has come."
-Victor Hugo-

Develop your ideas

Did you know that everything made or conceived starts with an idea? Ideas are the results of images provoked by your thought process and imagination. Ideas, in short, are *thoughts with an action*. They are the engine behind your innermost thoughts. Ideas drive the world and improve mankind. You can consciously make a decision to utilize your own ideas correctly, making them a key to bettering your life.

Don't limit yourself by thinking you don't have some great ideas. It just takes exercising your greatest muscle, your mind, to bring them to the forefront. Some research has said that the average person has at least four ideas a year that can make them wealthy.

That includes you. Think about it. Have you ever awakened in the middle of the night with that fantastic thought? Instead of acting on it, you decided to wait until morning to act or write it down, only to discover the thought was gone from your mind forever? A few years later, as you're flipping channels on the television, you run across some product being marketed on an infomercial. You look on in disbelief, saying to your family and friends that the product on television was really your idea.

Believe me when I tell you, there is power in your thoughts, even more than you realize. But the power alone does no good, without your developing subconscious thoughts into conscious ideas and taking action along with the follow-through. The idea will never materialize, eventually becoming nothing more than a fleeting memory.

Even when everything is going right and you are at the top of your career, you should always find time to investigate a new idea, thought or circumstance. I learned this lesson the hard way. At one time, I was doing so well that although I often had ideas about other projects, I constantly ignored them. Instead of following my subconscious ideas and making them conscious action, I avoided trying things, simply opting for the opportunities I was already familiar with.

I had spent a decade working in corporate America, trying to blend in and climb the same corporate ladder as everyone else. I achieved great success during that time by becoming a corporate sales superstar. I worked for two Fortune 500 companies, and became the number-one salesperson in the country for a division of one of the premier companies in the world. I met and sold to some of the most wonderful clients. My positions, skills and training allowed me to sell by learning and implementing the latest sales strategies and to assist and train salespeople in the latest techniques offered in the field of selling.

As I mentioned earlier, in one sense, I felt like the world was at my feet. I had made tremendous strides since those earlier years of living in that South Side Chicago housing development. Compared with those early years of my marriage, my personal life and family financial outlook had improved dramatically. Donna and I were traveling regularly through company perks, and on our own. Before we had turned thirty years old, we were traveling to places I had only dreamed of going, such as Hawaii and Puerto Rico; we even took a dream vacation through Europe on the world-famous Orient Express. Our family had now grown to three wonderful children, and included a family dog.

Now, you might ask, "What was the problem?" Most people would feel a sense of accomplishment or satisfaction in what they had achieved. I loved what I did, but never felt completely at ease, because I knew I had more to offer to the world, my community and my existence. In some ways, I had a calling from my heart to do even more. I wanted to do things that would outlive my existence on this earth.

In the personal and professional development training seminars I presently conduct around the country, I meet many participants who raise the same issues about their subconscious ideas that I once felt. They often share with me the fact that their nine-to-five jobs are not their source of happiness, or the thing that makes them feel valuable-it's simply a means to an end. Most of them agree that their value comes from doing things they are passionate about, and allows them to help others. That passion, along with a belief in what they're doing brings a level of esteem and accomplishment unsurpassed by any nine-to-five job. By not having this passion or ability to practice their ideas, a level of frustration sets in because they feel they could do better, live happier and accomplish more.

I had also seen my older brother Eddie get disillusioned while working for someone else. Regardless of what you or I feel, the person that signs the check gets the last word. At first, I thought I could avoid those pitfalls, because I personally had a great ten-year career up to that point.

But in the blink of an eye, I was assigned a new manager, and he had a limited vision of himself, which extended into a limited vision of my potential and the potential of my co-workers.

As quickly as he came on the scene, my corporate visions and plans started to become dimmer. As the time passed, I became uneasy with my position in corporate America. I kept playing in my mind what Eddie had taught me: not to get too comfortable on somebody else's job.

Practice Points:
- Ideas are thoughts with an action
- Use your greatest muscle, your mind

"Ideas are funny little things.
They won't work unless you do."
–unknown-

A thought with no action

I turned to Donna with an idea. The idea originated from what my brother Eddie always preached about having your own business. The more we decided it was time to start working toward having our own business, the more that idea excited us. We started to weigh our options, while growing restless about our future. We started brainstorming and researching different types of businesses that suited our tastes. A close friend had left corporate America to go into the fast-food business. So, after long consideration, we decided to try our hand in buying a similar fast-food franchise. We found the one we were interested in and did months of research. But after several failed attempts of finding the location we wanted, the idea gave way to disappointment.

I began to settle in again and hope that maybe my job would just work out. I crawled back into a hole of contentment, satisfied with what I was doing. I knew I was slowly growing miserable, but I was willing to take the abuse because it seemed less painful than following up on more ideas.

Again, you have to do more than have the idea. That's just the beginning. You have to follow the idea to the end of the earth with action. Because when you stop pursuing the idea, it dies.

List some ideas you have and never acted on.

1._____.
2._____.
3._____.

Here are some questions to ask and answer before you read on:

- Think back over your life and ask yourself, what have I done with the ideas I've had?
- Did those ideas give you a boost of energy and excitement?

Practice Points:
- Everything starts from an idea
- Everyone has at least four ideas a year
- Find your passion
- Ideas are thoughts with an action

Productive moments

Let's recap the principles you've incorporated into your life so far, in order to practice what you preach.: 1. Start where you are now to have a foundation. 2. Follow your life's philosophy by allowing your principles and values to dictate your morals, then follow up on your idea with action. In order to take those action steps to generate positive results, you'll need to set aside time in order to develop a plan around that idea. The fact that you are developing a process for success is authorizing your subconscious mind to adopt these principles as a way for you to experience ultimate results. In other words, you are reinforcing your own success, by not only talking, but doing.

A critical step to making your ideas work is mastering the art of time and allowing enough of it from your hectic schedule to start the process of planning. In planning, you'll need to regulate what I call *proactive well-timed moments.* These proactive well-timed moments are the time you allot and allow yourself to make available in the best time to spend planning. This is not the planning or the plan itself: we are talking about sacrificing to make available the time to sit down and plan. This step is crucial, because you'll recognize that your most valued resource is time itself. And to have more time, will take readjusting your schedule; for example, sacrificing some television time. In the long run, you will need to use good time management techniques to help propel your ideas onto a successful course.

I must admit, there is something about spending time alone that intimidates most people. But I want to point out that spending time alone and being alone are two different scenarios. I'm not asking you to spend idle time feeling sorry for yourself, or being non- productive. I'm talking about time designated in your life for uninterrupted planning, reflecting and developing. Being engaged in active, creative and constructive thinking is said to be one of the most difficult tasks for a human being. However, it is necessary in order to plan out those ideas and to think about how, why and when they can be implemented and utilized for your success. So stop now and schedule some time.

Now that you've committed to the time, there are some other factors about the time you need to acknowledge to make the process work. First, you have to slow down in mind and body to put yourself in a relaxed state of peak imagination and performance. For instance, you've heard some people talk about time seeming to move so slowly, while others complain about how time went by so quickly they weren't able to accomplish anything. You need to find out when time seems to move slower. That is usually when you are operating at your best, your most creative and alert parts of day or night. Don't gear this particular time to wonder, but to thinking constructively toward plans and manifesting your ideas for the future.

That incorporates spending time only reviewing your own thoughts. Don't be discouraged during this stage if you find that you don't truly know what it is you want. Don't give up and start sharing your thoughts and ideas with others just yet, taking away from your true sense of self. Letting others in too early can only rob you of your unique identity of thoughts and even your own potential concepts for greatness. You have to unequivocally know for yourself what you want, because if you don't, others will somehow shape you and your ideas into what they think and want. By doing this, you will have given up the right that God gave you-the right to choose for yourself.

There is a second reason I urge you to go through this stage alone and not give in to becoming so frustrated or busy that you give your idea to someone else: by giving it away, you may find your life's journey not being as fulfilled because now it's not uniquely yours.

After the idea has surfaced and the plan is developed, then you can invite others into your process. The most important thing to remember is that if your idea simply stays in your head and never sees action, it never becomes anything more than a fantasy. Once you start to manifest it, is when it becomes reality. When your time is well spent, it will help decide the rest of your life. You will have a purity of thought that will empower you.

Put down the best and most productive time of the day for yourself, a.m. or p.m._____

_____.

Practice Points:
- Readjust your schedule for planning time
- Think constructively
- Choose the most productive part of the day for your planning

Slow down to speed up

Because we were a two-income family with three small children, Donna and I found ourselves not having the time to plan. After work, I was responsible for picking up my oldest daughter, Deanna, from the after-school program, while Donna picked the younger two, Mario and Niki, from the babysitters, then headed home. Once home, after driving through Chicago's traffic, the mad dash started with Donna and me trying to get dinner ready, helping with homework, changing diapers and playing with the kids. They were adorable, and they wanted to spend every moment with us that they could, often until ten or eleven o'clock at night, and sometimes until midnight. You can imagine the way we felt the next morning, waking up at 5:30 a.m., starting this routine all over again. We found ourselves dragging to work, often worn down and half asleep from the night before, not to mention that the kids were cranky and tired. And finally, Donna and I were spending very little personal time together.

This day-to-day grind left us absolutely no time or energy to talk about things that could take us to the next level. We were not discussing the things of importance, like financial or spiritual needs, or just things about our future in general. Days seemed to turn into months, with us having no form of meaningful communication. This scenario could leave even the best couples stressed, pressured and frustrated.

Like many of you reading this now, I didn't know what to do and just figured that these were the grunt years, a reality of our relationship and lifestyle.

While at work, I casually introduced my family dilemma to a co-worker who had children a few years older than mine. He shared how his family had experienced similar frustrations when their children were younger. He and his wife decided to try a new routine that I call *the family saver*, which made certain their children were in bed by 7:30 p.m. He said it was the answer to their prayers because it allowed his children adequate sleep, while simultaneously allowing him and his wife more time.

I came home with this new idea that could save us time and relieve frustration. Donna was skeptical, because she didn't want the children to throw temper tantrums, but we decided to try it anyway. My co-worker warned me of the possibility of the kids revolting against the new rules, at least for a few days, opting to stay up. Our children did exactly that, kicking and crying to stay up. The crying almost made us give in and let them stay up or jump in the bed with us. We stayed focused however and within one week they were acclimated to the schedule. The new routine gave us an extra two or three hours at night to get more things done.

It gave us the time to slow down and catch our breath. Once rested, the extra time became invaluable, giving us a chance to plan and strategize.

This simple but revolutionary suggestion worked so well, we decided to share its results with other couples experiencing the same phenomenon. Time after time, before we could fully explain how and why it worked, we were interrupted with all the excuses of why it wouldn't work in their case. We soon came to the conclusion that people complain to complain, not to change their situation. In fact, it's easier to make an excuse for a situation than to search for a solution and then implement that solution. Don't find your life in between what you really want in your heart, and what you settle for because of lack of knowledge, skill, and desire-all of which can stop you from actually achieving. Start with deciding you're ready to slow down the pace to spend some time figuring out your future and, more important, plotting your destiny. The results of the time that came available for us became invaluable; we had more time to read, develop hobbies and plan more financial matters.

Preach Points:
- Plan during the grunt years
- Put your children on a productive schedule/family saver
- Share your results with friends and family

The success plan

Now that you have been mindful of putting time in your schedule to plan, you're ready to understand the importance of the plan itself. A plan is the thought-out design or scheme to get you to the end or desired result. Although you're seeking an end result, the true key to a successful plan is to have the ability to *constantly change and adjust* what you're doing along the way to make it better. This allows you the opportunity to see the plan work, and to constantly improve it while you are enjoying the journey. This important theory of constant change and adjustment is often overlooked in many plans, causing people to give up in the beginning stages. The beginning and subsequent stages of a plan can look bleak and unenjoyable.

This theory is often missing in one of the most significant plans you can ever make: the plan of sharing your life in marriage with someone you love. You've heard the saying that couples spend more time planning a wedding day than they spend planning the marriage life. The excitement of anticipating the perfect day, which includes family and friends, can leave many couples in shock once the actual wedding ends and the marriage begins. Some couples never discuss the constant change and adjustment needed for a long lifetime of commitments. The marriage becomes a chore instead of a shared journey. The couple is married and divorced before they ever understood that the marriage had to be worked on daily, getting constant improvement and upgrades. Both parties have to want the enjoyment and the growth in the relationship.

Other parts of the marriage plan that need constant adjustments include handling finances, how the children will be raised spiritually and a host of other considerations going well past the original wedding day.

I've heard many people pose the question, Why plan? As one lady went so far as to express to me in a workshop, "You're going to die one day anyway." One workshop participant said, "I can't tell what's going to happen in my future, so why think about it?" Now these arguments might seem to make sense on the surface, but I'll tell you, these excuses can become huge cop-outs for you, and eliminate a vehicle for your success. In essence, your plan becomes a blueprint that leads to your goals, dreams, desires and success.

Another way to look at planning is like taking a trip. While planning that trip, you need to have a destination. Without a destination, you may take a drive, but you wouldn't know where you're going. You want to know where you're going in order to determine how much money you'll need, what clothes you'll need to pack, how long you'll stay and, most important, when you are coming back.

A life plan gives you the same important tools and information you need to navigate your life. The plan simply says, "This is what I'm going to do and this is how I'm going to do it." The plan also gives you an opportunity to measure where you should be, at what time and at what point. Remember, at some point you'll look back on your life and realize this life wasn't a trial run. Don't regret that you didn't have more time. Don't end up wishing you could do this thing called life over again. For you, your second chance is now.

By giving yourself an opportunity to have a plan, you have the flexibility to adjust the plan as needed each day. Planning also gives you accountability, along with a way of measuring your progress by breaking down the big picture each and every day.

Besides having a plan, you need the right plan that will work for you. Imagine leaving for California from Chicago but having a map of New York. You would be frustrated because none of the roads on the New York map would lead to California. You could give it your best effort, but because you have the wrong map, you can't make it to your final destination. Even if you followed this map at full speed, you'd just get to the wrong destination twice as fast. In order to succeed, you'll need to find the right plan. It gives you the best map to your destination.

You may ask, "How do you know if the plan is feasible?" To find out if the plan is feasible, you'll have to practice constant change and adjustment to get what you say you want. For example, you have to ask yourself a number of questions, and the questions have to be detailed. Don't sell yourself short by asking unclear questions, and don't settle for unclear answers.

In other words, without the right questions, your mind can't conceive the right answers. The questions put the challenge to you, and the answers are you. A famous quote says, "Shoot for the moon, so if you fall short you'll still be amongst the stars." Dream big! That's simply called "having a vision." The Bible teaches us that where there is no vision, the people perish.

Let's go back to when my brother Eddie asked me how much was I worth. Although I was twenty-three years old and making fifty dollars a week, I had to begin thinking like a person making $50,000 a year. You and I have to visualize the largeness of our future long before we get there.

Practice Points:
- A successful plan will express continuous action steps
- Not planning can eliminate your success path
- A plan gives you a final destination

Passion first, plan second

I mentioned earlier that Donna and I decided to open a fast-food restaurant, but it didn't work out. The reason we were so high on a restaurant business was because our good friends were doing very well in their franchise. It was their passion to be in that industry but it was not ours. When we started looking at the long hours it would take to keep the restaurant open, both Donna and I knew we didn't have the desire, no matter how good the money seemed. That explains why our idea for opening up a fast-food restaurant failed. In order for our plan to work, we would have had to confront the question of whether the restaurant business was a passion in our heart, soul and mind. In other words, we had a plan but we were using the wrong map.

Just as for us, your true burning desire has to come from something that keeps you excited when you start to visualize it. The questions we discussed earlier in this chapter are the same questions I had to ask myself to help me uncover my true passions. My own passions were deep inside me. After probing myself with the right questions, I knew I had a desire to write about the lives of two of my dearest childhood friends, Ray Anthony Grandberry and Garry "Deke" Kennedy.

The reason I wanted to write about Ray stemmed from the friendship we had growing up in the projects. Like most kids raised in the ghetto, Ray and I had a dream to make it out and become baseball and football stars. As a small boy, Ray could sense something was wrong with the neighborhood and the environment we were growing up in. So he wanted to write a book about our experiences, both good and bad. As early as eight years old, he talked about writing this book, which he'd say would end with us being the heroes and winning the fame and glory. He talked about this book to me so often, that even as a kid, I started believing in his dream.

As with Ray, my experiences with Deke helped to mold me into the man I am today. I met Deke at our high school, called Lindblom Technical High School. I left my neighborhood at fourteen years old to attend this school, which at the time was the highest-ranking academic public school in Chicago. Unfortunately, the school was located in the South Side's Englewood neighborhood, the second-worst crime ridden community in the inner city. Because the gangs and violence were so prevalent in the community, it left students like us vulnerable to the vices and destruction of the gangs. Deke and I became protectors of each other to escape those dangers of the community every day. He also became my best friend when Momma left home during my teen-age years. I was fascinated by his ability to captivate and motivate his peers and friends alike. Deke was a man among boys with his keen sense and thirst for knowledge.

Both Ray and Deke eventually met each other through me, as we all enrolled at the same college. Deke's life ended on that college campus. Ray's life ended six years later in the South Side neighborhood we had grown up in. Both of them experienced tragic endings to their promising lives long before they reached their thirtieth birthdays.[5] To write about them, I was compelled to include the stories and tragic deaths of many others whose lives shaped the way we thought, acted and reacted.

I often found myself sharing with others the stories of our lives. Even on my corporate job, I'd often share Ray's and Deke's overwhelming desire and odds to make it out of the inner city. Then, I would share how their lives motivated me to excel in sports and then, in corporate sales. Those conversations would always have the people listening spellbound.

I enchanted co-workers by exceeding their expectations of me. I knew I had come a long way and was the first to realize I had developed into an individual with unique talents. By putting a success system around that talent, it would continually allow me to operate above the circumstances that existed in my earlier life. I created new paradigms for myself by creating the world I wanted to live in instead of the world that I knew once existed. My uniqueness was becoming my greatest friend. This brings me to the point that after you have a plan, get others involved by telling as many people about what you are trying to do. This will help you get to others who can help you.

---

[5] Read more about Ray and Deke's life in "Silent Cry" parts I, II, III & IV

- Have a burning desire
- Operate above your circumstances

Create your luck

I also knew that good things weren't just happening because I was in the right place at the right time. So many people have believed in the notion that people who are successful just hit streaks of good luck. In reality, successful people will tell you their *luck* occurred when their *preparation plus hard work met an opportunity*. In other words, you have to be prepared consciously and work very hard to create the opportunities that you are prepared to receive. The bottom line is that in order to succeed, *you have to push the issue with hard work.* It's not about winging your life or its outcome. It's about having a plan that puts you in a position to take full advantage of the opportunities when they present themselves.

The thought of writing a book burned deep inside of me and would often take over my subconscious thought process from time to time. But instead of pursuing the book idea, Donna and I tried the food franchise. It didn't pan out because my heart wasn't in it. So I made an adjustment to my plan. If plan A doesn't work, you should have an alternative, plan B.

Just as I moved to plan B, my brother Eddie approached me with his new idea. Eddie had been talking for a few years about going into the clothing industry. As long as I could remember, he had been a fancy dresser, with an eye for clothes. Eddie decided it was time to leave his accounting business behind and move on to his next dream. His plan was to open a men's suit and tie shop. But first, he would start small by selling just shirts. By this time, we hadn't worked together for over ten years. I'll never forget the night Eddie came to my house to pitch his idea. He assumed I wanted to be part of his idea that included us selling shirts right out of the trunk of our cars. I stopped Eddie in midsentence and said to him, " I have no intention of selling shirts out of my car." He left that night with the strangest look on his face. I had already been down that road and knew that selling clothes wasn't my passion. I love my brother, but I had to make a stand. The only thought that motivated me was the idea of writing a book. I felt I had a window of opportunity, and if I didn't act on it, I'd lose the desire as the detailed memories of my friends would start fading away. The same is true for you. If you don't act on your own idea, you may lose desire and focus.

But even though I had a desire to write a book, I still didn't make a clear decision to move on with the book idea. Instead, I procrastinated and continued to allow my corporate manager to dictate my future. His negative actions were getting into my head and making me miserable. I began losing confidence, while becoming mentally discouraged and drained. In the back of my mind, I was not moving on the book idea because I was afraid. Writing a book meant I had to start all over, and I didn't know anything about the writing industry.

Now brainstorm some options you can utilize to make your plan work. Here are some questions you should answer to help make your plan more obvious.

1. What is your passion ?_____.
2. What is stopping you from doing what is passionate?____
_____.

Preach Points:
- Luck is when preparation plus hard work meets an opportunity
- Your uniqueness is your greatness
- Have a plan B

3. Operate Out of Your Values and Principles

"Watch your thoughts, they become words. Watch your words, they become actions. Watch your actions, they become habits. Watch your habits, they become character. Watch your character, it becomes your destiny."

-Unknown-

Know thy self

By answering the previous questions, in the last chapter, you know your plan should be focused totally around your ideas and passions. The plan should incorporate the ideas you feel passionate about, whether it's starting a business, getting a promotion or losing weight. By having the plan, you become more aware of your strengths, shortcomings and limitations. You also have the power to consciously make sure your plan is built on the proper values and principles.

Remember, the results your plan nets are based on integrity, honesty, truth and other moral standards. Living by your *moral standards* gives you the fortitude, strength and self-determination to commit to the things that are most passionate to you. Great societies have impacted the world by applying truths guided by principles for everyday living. This allowed these societies to find peace, happiness and prosperity.

Your personal plan can have the same potency, while netting you remarkable results if it's driven by truth. By being rooted in the strength of truth, you will believe in its deep sense of ethical purpose. That purpose will allow you to commit to doing great works that will ultimately outlive your own existence.

Truth is absolute. It doesn't change. So by developing your plan from a sense of truth, values and principles, you'll be guaranteed the solid foundation from which to work. However, most people are not building a plan on the right foundation or by using the right material. A simple illustration would be to try constructing a building (plan) without having a solid foundation or proper building material (truth, ethics, etc.). The private school my three children once attended recently constructed a new church. Before they started building the church, the blueprint containing all of the specifications (plans) had to be approved. If the church had been built with faulty material or on shaky ground, it would have eventually fallen down. The church plan and your personal plan have to have the right ingredients and a solid foundation to stand the test of time.

After you have the right plan with the right ingredients, you have to share the plan with others. The plan has to be shared with the builders because they have to be trusted to bring the proper materials. This is where many people stumble when trying to get their plan off the ground. They can't seem to trust others enough to bring the right ingredients. Because they have a *scarcity mentality*, their plans, hopes and dreams start to disappear into a distant memory. Remember to trust your intuitive feelings about others who share the same values you share.

I made the decision to make my idea a reality. In doing so, I had to immediately try to trust others. I had to look for information, encouragement, or advice from people who knew something about writing books. This didn't mean I wasn't afraid or even intimidated because I knew that I didn't have a clue about writing. So I based my trust on the fact that I had a plan that carried values. This gave me a foundation to go out and ask others carrying the same values for some information.

It's easier to give advice than to follow it, especially when it's following your own advice. I began struggling to believe in my own concept about presenting my ideas with confidence and surety. Like most of us, I knew in principle I was right. That fact should have propelled me to speak about my plan with confidence. But that was easier said than done. In the back of my mind, I'd often think, *Even if I could write a book, who was going to actually read it?*

Finally, to take some pressure off myself, I convinced myself that I could use a ghost writer. I inquired at church, on college campuses and with family members, and they all advised me to write it myself. That thought was still too intimidating, because that meant I had to put all the responsibility for writing on myself.

I brought my idea of writing to Eddie and he suggested I call a man in Chicago named Dempsey Travis. Mr. Travis is a respected real-estate broker who has written many books about African-American Chicago history.

I put a token phone call into his office, assuming I wouldn't get through to him, but his receptionist connected me. A bit stunned, I said, "Mr. Travis, this is E.J. Bassette. I'm interested in writing a book about my life story..." He stopped me in midsentence and asked, "Son, how old are you?"

As I told him my age, he shouted, "How are you going to write an autobiography. You're too young, and you definitely don't have anything to say!" I became so intimidated, that I agreed with him.

He took over the phone conversation and shared with me that he didn't write his first book until the age of forty-five, after he had traveled and fought in the Second World War. I was practically in tears at this point. In a desperate plea, I asked what he thought about my pursuing a ghost writer? In a more irritated tone, he said he knew for sure that I wasn't serious about writing a book. "Son," he said, "if you were serious, you would pick up a pen and the words would flow from your hand as if it was music to your ears." Then he said in a hurried voice, "You've taken enough of my time," and hung up the phone. I stood at that phone booth in total disbelief. I was moved to tears, until the shock wore off. Then my anger set in. I became so upset that I convinced myself I would write this book to prove him wrong. A speaker by the name of Willie Jolley once said, "Success is a failure that got mad." And that day, I was mad enough to get motivated.

I took notes of our conversation and looked for the positives in what he said. I did find the one positive thing I needed to hear: "If you were serious, you would pick up a pen and the words would flow from your hand as if it was music to your ears." I knew he was telling the truth about that, so that statement became my rallying cry. Up to that point, I had been making excuses about writing. I just didn't really think I could write a book. His words became part of my paradigm shift and my truth. I used him and his words as a way to throw myself a challenge. Sometimes, we don't want to hear the truth. But after that phone call, I did begin to write a little.

Preach points:
- Build on solid foundation (truth)
- Don't have a scarcity mentality
- A success is a failure that got mad

"There is no right way to do something wrong."
-Unknown-

Create your environment

Once you operate your plan in truth, you'll become extremely conscious of the high standards you've set in your life. By staying in line consistently with those new standards, your environment will become more tailored for the *inner peace*, thus producing a more *fruitful existence*. The empowerment to give your plan all you've got will begin to manifest itself. In other words, the truth shall set you free, and you'll function with a sense of urgency, sincerity and happiness because you are following the principles you believe one hundred percent.

On the other side, many people are disgruntled and insincere with their own actions, because they can't seem to operate with the values and principles needed. They continually find their lives in a rut, ignoring those standards that are available to them to bring about a more fulfilling life. The solution seems so close, but yet so far. In an effort to help, let's define what it is most people are searching for, and why. They are searching for an intangible feeling called happiness. Most people tend to associate happiness with pleasure and sadness with pain.

Think about yourself when you're happy. It truly comes into your life when your thoughts and actions are consistent with your beliefs. Then those beliefs have to be carried out daily to bring on the happiest state. So you associate the feeling with the experience of the feeling. For example, you often hear very successful salespeople talk about their belief in what they're doing or the product they're selling. That belief gives them a strong conviction to push themselves to sell their product with confidence.

Their belief is that others are truly benefiting from the product or service. This allows them to feel good, thus bringing about success and ultimate happiness.

You can change your environment by making positive conscious decisions reflecting your true beliefs. The more you follow your beliefs, the more you'll see life as a happy, positive experience.

The reason your world might be suffering at this point is that you have the wrong belief system, thus producing the wrong results. Find yourself and you'll find your world can be full of inner joy and fruitful existence. James Barrie said it this way, "The secret of happiness is not in doing what one likes, but in liking what one does."

Practice Points:
- Become conscious of your high standards
- Keep your thoughts and actions consistent with your beliefs
- Believe what you want will benefit you and others

"One of life's most painful moments comes when
we must admit that we didn't do our homework, that
we are not prepared."
-Merlin Olsen-

<u>Never too young to learn</u>

Searching for happiness is a major challenge that affects adults, as well as young people trying to give their lives more meaning, direction and purpose. Remember, when you're not living with an awareness of values or principles, your environment seems to spiral out of control, regardless of age.

You witness or hear about the unhappiness first-hand. Many of our youth are faced with their lives not going in accordance with the principles and values of the universe. You *can't do evil* and *experience happiness*. I learned this lesson back in the eighties when I attended college. My dream was to pursue a professional football career. That in itself was fine, because outwardly I had goals.

The problems came in the lifestyle I chose while attaining those goals. I was not living in accordance with the moral standards I had been taught to follow. I knew better, but I allowed my moral standards to decline. But I still expected to receive good things including happiness, regardless of the way I conducted myself. I didn't truly appreciate the principle that says what you put into life is what you truly get back.

Sports added a *false paradigm*. As an athlete, I thought of myself as being physically invincible and indestructible. That attitude was fine on the football field where the objective became to seek and destroy the opponent. But off the field, that same reckless attitude caused all types of problems.

Outwardly, I showed an air of cockiness, which was really misplaced confidence, while inside, I felt empty and nervous and suffered from low self- esteem. That lack of confidence resulted in my not valuing the ramifications of my actions. By not respecting my values, I managed to get a young lady pregnant before I turned twenty years old. This action left me confused, unhappy, misguided and lonely.

Outwardly, I still managed to falsely convince myself that by chasing the dream of football, I could somehow be cheered by fans and alleviate the pain and mistakes. I figured the success of the game would wipe away all the unhappiness I had caused in my life and the lives of other people.

My lack of values and principles didn't just affect my football career and personal life. But it affected my grades, because I had not practiced academic discipline and didn't have the grade point average to get accepted into the department of my choice. During my last year in football, my hopes of playing professional football disappeared, leaving my life in disarray.

Instead of living my life of moral standards leading to a source of happiness, I was confused and on the verge of flunking out of school. I blamed everyone for my problems but myself. I knew that going back home to the inner city of Chicago without a college degree meant finding nothing but the decaying housing development where more and more people were falling prey to the viciousness of drugs and hopelessness of unemployment. I wasn't consciously trained on how to fully take advantage of my opportunities, so I sat in my dorm room in despair, feeling the emptiness of belonging neither at school or at home. I had to find something that could give me hope.

Many of the peers I confided in were in a similar or even worse situation. There was too much fighting, drinking, sex and partying for most of us to see through the array of misplaced values. Most good students were left to fend for themselves, and the others were falling into the big black hole, flunking out and heading home. I sank to my lowest academic level when I started taking easy college courses such as gym, basketball, and learning the rules of the library course. I was officially making myself an academic vegetable.

The whole college scene of cheating on tests, flunking classes, pregnancies, fighting, racial confrontations, and the possibility of sexually transmitted disease left mental scars on many of us who digested its terrible entrée.

I finally had enough and decided to slow down, wondering if it could get any worse. The realization of the lost feeling of sinking in quicksand was not given to me exclusively. But I became determined to pull myself out of its mess.

As the new semester started, two college professors took an interest in me as a person. They inspired me by believing I could be successful in their classes and in life. Both offered me a way to beat my circumstances with discipline, studying, working hard and using my mind.

Appealing to my mind and not my athletic ability, they instilled in me a sense of pride and offered some solutions for my turmoil. With renewed values, self-esteem and new-found study habits, the things that my parents taught me started to resurface. The change on the inside became evident as my peers noticed the change in my attitude, emotions and demeanor.

I began sharing my renewed value system and inner strength with anyone who cared to listen. Through sharing, I realized many of my peers weren't necessarily interested in the same level of consciousness.

I had a sense of urgency in teaching my friends the new way because the violence was escalating on campus. The campus body received a shock when my dear friend from high school, Garry "Deke" Kennedy, had an encounter that came to a bloody end. He was murdered in that college town, changing me and many of my peers forever.[6]

---

[6] For more on college life, read "Silent Cry" part III

In a salute to Garry, I vowed to mature into an individual who had a stronger appreciation for life with a desire to help others. That belief had to ultimately come from me and no one else. As with me, there are things that can change your life completely. Although these changes can be witnessed in an outward form, they all come from within the heart and soul. When your principles change, others will see the transformation before you open your mouth.

After Garry's death, I continued to find the courage to change by getting quiet enough to view my inner soul. I knew the changes I needed to make dealt with my spirit and not my physical being. After my inner spirit changed, other things that were more visible changed.

• Changing my academic priorities: I was nobody's dummy, and decided I didn't want to be viewed as one.

• Becoming a gentleman: I respected young ladies and gentlemen by choosing politeness over chaos.

• Focusing on graduating from college: I researched and found a program more suited for my career desires. I left sports behind and concentrated on my career.

• Taking responsibility for my life: As well as accepting the consequences, I also learned to stop blaming others.

By practicing what I preached relieved stress, and put me in a new frame of mind to focus on what was important. Going back to the Chicago projects as a failure, licking my wounds was no longer an option. I developed a plan, and it was based on principles and values. I stopped partying and started studying to fit more with my new standards of finishing school and achieving a college degree. As I began solving my problems on the campus, I began assisting other students with their problems. I also bonded with new friends who didn't seem to care for me before. I began showing up to every class on time. I started participating in class, taking notes and completing assignments.

This successful repetition of principles and values by constantly changing and adjusting became a focus for me to get out of college. For the first time, I became more competitive in the classroom than I was on the football field. This led to my biggest personal decision in college. I walked away from football to become a full-time student. As difficult as it seemed at the time, it changed me forever. I didn't have anyone to blame or commend for my future but myself. I began to depend on my own ability to fail or succeed. To this day, I motivate and coach college students in avoiding many of the pitfalls I experienced.

Admitting your faults and relieving your guilt allows you to leave the past behind.
Positive self talk and daily affirmations can help you.

1. I used to _____ but I've learned from those mistakes.
2. I used to _____ but now I'm a better person.

Preach Points
- Stop blaming others
- Don't carry misplaced confidence
- Become realistic about your future

Create lessons for success/Self Mastering

Regardless of what life experiences have given you the highest high or the lowest low, the lessons that came from those experiences will come in handy when other challenges arise. So once you've learned a valuable lesson, keep it in your *mental bank* as a constant reminder.

I had to remember the good and bad of those college memories, because the experiences still played an important part in my current success. You can also take your lessons and improve on them, by constantly changing and adjusting the results to make them better than before. Now, after a decade of sales success, my survival instincts were telling me to pay close attention to the handwriting on the wall. My sales territory was being changed as my manager was becoming overly critical of my performance.

Instead of going full speed ahead toward my dreams, I continued to coast, and stayed in what was becoming a toxic situation. I kept giving my manager the power to control my destiny and dictate my agenda. Then I'd let that control cause stress and pressure, leaving me upset and unable to look ahead clearly. Don't think I wasn't trying to make a move. I was passively talking to other managers and even human resources to get the concerns resolved. I loved the job I was doing, but the suffocating managing style he used was not promoting team spirit and leadership. When I went into my mental bank, I constantly reminded myself of what I enjoyed about my life and job.

When I wrote, I loved the feeling of expressing myself. I also enjoyed sharing information with others in my sales-training capacity. I loved making people's lives better personally and professionally. Sharing seemed to come naturally. I also freely gave information to young people I came into contact with-relevant information like avoiding drugs, crime and gangs, or how to get into college. Being a sales trainer allowed me the opportunity to share corporate strategies on business and selling. Everyone I trained rated my training style highly because I listened to them and trained them in a manner to fit their learning and behavioral style.

I first became interested in corporate speakers and trainers in the late eighties. I attended a seminar given by Tom Hopkins, one of the top sales trainers in the country. As 3,000 people filed into the convention hall to participate in his workshop, I found myself fascinated that 3,000 other people and I paid $100 to attend. My sales buddies and I pulled out our calculators and multiplied the $100 times 3000 people. We estimated the revenues at over \$300,000, not including books or tape sales.

After experiencing Tom Hopkins, I kept the idea of training in the back of my mind. My subconscious goal was to become the top trainer for my company, then eventually start my own training company sometime in the future. I worked hard to put myself in the top 10% of the elite salespeople in my company. I also wanted to become a national sales trainer for the company. But after accomplishing my sales goals, management denied my attempts for that promotion, and denied me opportunities into other management areas. So I went on to the second Fortune 500 company and started over to accomplish my plan. This time, to leave no doubt as to my ability, I became the number one salesperson in the country. After two companies and ten years of hard work, I figured my ticket had been stamped for approval. I pursued the national sales training position with the second company. Again, I was denied. Again I was not only being denied for that position, but for all other promotional opportunities. I fought for a token training position, as my new manager announced that he did not envision for me a corporate training position at any level.[7] But the desire to train, share and teach still burned inside of me.

Practice Points:
- Share what you believe
- Keep learning from your past experience
- Go to your mental bank for reminders

"Man's mind, once stretched by a
new idea, never goes back to its original shape."
-Oliver Wendell Holmes-

---

[7] Read "Silent Cry": part IV by E.J. Bassette

A one speech wonder/A speaker is born

It had now been years since I had been exposed to Tom Hopkins, one of the world's leading authorities on sales training. Even though I had experienced individual sales successes, all my larger visions were not being manifested. I couldn't seem to get my superiors to ever support my ambitions. This started to bring on undue stress, so to keep my sanity, I decided to speak in my spare time. For fun, I figured I'd dabble in speaking by donating time back to my old high school and attending career days. This would give me an opportunity to share techniques and information on how to survive in life and business.

But up to this point I didn't seek out other speakers. I didn't have a plan to learn the industry on my own. I still envisioned myself doing corporate training for my company. I continued to search for ways to bring management on board with my plans.

All that changed one evening as I started my commute home from work. While driving, I spotted a college campus billboard featuring a career-day speaker. I did a U-turn, figuring it would be interesting to hear what the speaker had to say.

Walking into the student auditorium, I noticed a few students were in a panic, while most sat in their chairs, anticipating an inspiring lecture. I approached a concerned student, and he explained that a dilemma had left one of their featured speakers unable to make the presentation. Without hesitating, I asked him what topic was the speaker going to discuss. When he told me, I volunteered to substitute for the speaker.

What did I have to lose? The room was already filled with students. The student in charge accepted my offer. I spoke to that auditorium of college students about success and corporate America. The students feasted on my words of encouragement.

At the end of the session I was enlightened and encouraged by my own words. I heard myself encourage them and it gave me a lift that was magical. Many of the students stayed around to continue the conversation after the lecture. The evening fit like a hand in a glove. I was so inspired because I had given the students some information they needed, and their thirst for knowledge was equaled by my desire to share.

One student, Deborah O. Brown, surprised me by requesting an interview for the campus newspaper. During the interview, the student treated me like a big-time speaker. She asked me what other projects I had on my agenda. I decided to share my ambition of writing a book and furthering my speaking career.

As I look back on that magical night, I recall four powerful things that happened from that experience.

- First, I was so excited to speak. Afterward, I experienced a natural high for weeks. I knew I needed that feeling of speaking again.

- Second, when I received the news article, it became the first time someone put in print what I dreamed about-actually writing a book. Seeing those words in print excited me to no end. I must have eventually read that article over a hundred times.

- Third, the article embarrassed me into action. I would let myself down, but I wasn't going to let the students down. That particular student never knew, until much later, how her small article helped motivate me to work toward one of my life dreams.

- Fourth, but not least, I met friends for life, some of the students, Scott Singleton and Michael Wortham, along with the featured speaker, Emily Means-Willis, still stay in touch until this day.

Preach points:
- Look for opportunities
- Be willing to help unconditionally
- Others will rally around your cause

Practice What You Preach

<u>Reality check</u>

Now, I wanted to pick up the pace. I decided to proactively search for opportunities to speak and train, as well as plan times to write. Though I considered these two of the toughest careers I could venture into, I still felt an overall need to find more opportunities to express what was on my mind. With my new consciousness, I decided to take the positive road, and actively pursue youth motivational speaking. I figured with my success in corporate America, along with being young, energetic and optimistic, every school would allow me an opportunity to speak to their youth.

I started targeting inner-city public school principals and teachers to see if I could donate time to speak to their students. I even asked my manager for a half-day opportunity to go into a community to donate time. To my surprise, both the schools and my management turned me down.

School officials wanted to see referrals and credentials, as well as other things that accompany a reputable speaker. They were asking for things that I couldn't give them. My manager suggested to upper management that I had lost my focus of sales, and possibly should look into becoming a social worker.

These incidents left me extremely disappointed and confused. In my mind, the school system was screaming for black men to stand up and get involved in the community. Corporate America preached community service and giving back as one of their missions. But when I tried, I was given the runaround. There is a saying, "If it was easy, everybody would be doing it." So I had to make a decision: Was I simply interested in speaking and writing, or was I really going to *become* a speaker and writer?

I realized I didn't have enough credibility, meaning I had to go back to the drawing board to make it work. Another part of me wanted to give up and quit. "Who was I fooling?" I thought "I'm just a wannabe with a few pages of notes, calling them a book." I had only one speech to claim a speaking career.

I had absolutely no credentials in the speaking or writing fields. The fact was that everything I knew had brought me to the place where I was. Now I had to make a choice. There is a life equation that says, *What you know + what you do = What you earn.* If you're not comfortable with where you are, you have to face the reality that: *To earn more, you have to learn more.* In my case, although I had accumulated numerous sales awards and training accomplishments in corporate America, I had absolutely nothing to show as a speaker or writer that I could use to promote myself.

It usually happens that way. We take for granted the years of time and dedication it takes people to achieve a high level of success in mastering their craft. When we decide this is something we want for ourselves, we think we can jump past all the hoops, training and experience. We expect all the doors to immediately open for us because we sincerely want to succeed.

There is a name for this phenomenon; it's called the *instant gratification stage,* or the *I want it and I want it now syndrome.* This syndrome causes us to behave like little children, stomping our feet, taking our ball and going home when we don't get our way. I tried not to take what was happening personally. I looked for the lessons and tried to gut them out. I learned it takes incredible fortitude, concentration and desire to focus during the difficult times to get what you want. Now I had to apply this lesson again in order to accomplish my goal.

1.Proactively search for opportunities: As we said before, "Preparation plus hard work creates opportunities." Seek them out. Don't let them seek you out.

2.Build a reputation: By your having the proper credentials, people will appreciate your talent.

3.Learn more to earn more: If you are not where you want to be economically, you're not valued enough in your industry, additional training might be necessary.

4.Be patient: Patience is a virtue. Learn to be steady and consistent.

Preach Points
- Be aware of the instant gratification stage
- Don't take experiences for granted
- You gain experience by doing

"Rather fail with honor than succeed by fraud."
-Sophocles-

Making a comeback

I knew I needed to acquire a strong educational foundation in both the speaking and writing fields. To have people trust me in these respective fields, they had to hear good things about my work. I decided to research both markets, including asking anyone I could to help or share information. I needed to stop playing around with my plans, and just go full speed ahead.

Like me, you may have a tendency to dabble in things that you claim you want and need to accomplish. Dabbling with your life's dream is not a commitment and will only delay you from reaching the level you desire. Anthony Robbins, author of *Awaken the Giant Within*, states that most people mistake having an *interest* in something for making a decision to *do* something. A commitment has to be a full-fledged decision to see something through to the end.

To get from point A to point B, to get from thinking to doing, to go from a dream to reality, all deal with the challenge of knowing what you want and staying on course. By staying on course, I needed to work on my skills all the time, every day. That meant fighting my own limited vision, and going to find ways to speak and train others consistently. The same is true for your endeavors. You have to challenge yourself to do what you believe in each and every day. Just the thought of what that would take may overwhelm you to exhaustion. So make sure you put it in your plan.

Preach Points:
- Research the market
- Challenge yourself on a daily basis
- Fight to stay on course daily

Second time around

It had been six months since I made the speech to that first college group. I had to prove to myself that I wasn't just a one-speech wonder. I finally encouraged another group of college students to allow me to speak. This was different because it was my first speech after consciously and officially declaring myself a motivational speaker. The group couldn't pay me a fee, but they were giving me an opportunity to address the students on campus. More important, I decided this was the career I wanted to pursue. You may have heard, "If you tell enough people what you do or what you're trying to do, sooner or later someone is going to believe you." In other words, they're going to call your bluff.

That's how I got this speaking engagement. I mentioned to a college student that I was a speaker and she insisted I come to her campus to speak. She even arranged the meeting area and organized the event. You see, I started telling everybody I was a speaker. Now that I had really opened my big mouth, I was not really telling a lie. I was just passionate when I talked to other people about speaking as a career.

I was still struggling with my job, but I knew I had to start somewhere. Up to this point, I was still reciting my best speeches in the shower. Now that I was convinced, I wanted to speak and write more than anything else.

Ready to make my mark, I drove with Eddie two hours to that campus. I had practiced my speech for days. The student and her organization promoted the event well, because students came from all over the campus to hear what I had to say.

As I walked to the podium, my adrenaline flowed and I became uncontrollably nervous. Then, before I started to speak, my mind went blank. My confidence disappeared. To make matters worse, my notes suddenly looked like a foreign language. For the next hour and thirty minutes, I held the notes close to my face. Occasionally, I managed to say something that made the audience chuckle. When I looked up to see their faces, I'd lose my place.

This forced me to repeatedly apologize to the audience. During the speech, I mistakenly made an inappropriate joke about people being overweight. There were oversized ladies in the audience who were offended and thought I had purposely singled them out. When the audience looked at them and laughed, it made things worse. By the end of my presentation, over half the audience had already left. When I finally ended, the feedback was even more discouraging than the speech.

I thought some people stayed around just to see me driven out of town by the angry mob. The feedback from the audience was that I came off as arrogant and insensitive. Most stated that they didn't want me to come back to speak to their group again.

There were two choices I could make after that speech: I could hang my head and give up, or I could shake off the dust and get back up and do it again. I decided I wasn't going to humiliate and frustrate myself again. That day taught me that I wasn't as good as I thought I was. I also learned not to believe that press clipping about myself. I had a lot of hard work to do. Just because I tried to do what I believed in didn't mean I did it the most effective way. It also didn't mean everybody in the audience would agree with me. Now I had to find the courage to get up and speak in front of an audience again, knowing there was a possibility I could fall flat on my face again.

Preach Points:
- Say it enough and others will believe you
- Don't believe your own press clippings
- Learn from your feedback

"Don't want what others have, but learn what they did to get it and earn your own."
-E.J. "Edge" Bassette-

A Dance with Greatness: A Lesson from Michael Jordan

I kept grasping for positive life lessons and stories to keep myself focused during the transition of working a job I was starting to hate to doing what I envisioned my future to hold. Remember, we discussed earlier that once you've learned a valuable lesson, keep it in your *mental bank* as a reminder. Then constantly adjust and improve on it to get better results the next time.

I also knew that perseverance was going to be a key to establishing this new venture. I've learned that school and education can get you a job, but it's self-education and self discipline that makes you rich. Formal education teaches you theory and task-oriented functions, such as how to follow directions and to follow up. But *self- education* teaches you and me how to survive in this world, by dealing with others and developing a hunger and thirst for success. With a combination of formal education (book smarts) and self- education (street smarts), I knew then that I could one day be *unstoppable* as a speaker and writer.

Through media such as television, newspapers and the Internet, you and I are exposed daily to unstoppable people who have already achieved high levels of greatness. Because we don't know them personally, it doesn't always occur to us what great lessons we could learn from them if we took the time to dig into their mental bank.

I learned one of those valuable lessons in, of all places, a dance club on the South Side of Chicago. This particular lesson dates back to the mid-eighties, before Michael Jordan was married. In the early years of his Bull's career, Michael was known to come to the South Side and hang out at a few of the nightclubs. I would often stop off at a club called The Cotton Club after work to meet friends and do a little partying before heading home.

The Cotton Club is a middle-class hangout known for good music and good people. Once the music started, I asked a few of the prettier ladies in the club to dance, but they all turned me down without a second look. As I stood against a far wall, rejected, I noticed this same group of ladies turning away every other man who approached them for a dance. Suddenly a buzz started in the club, as Michael Jordan of the Chicago Bulls, along with Wilbur Marshall, Pro Bowl linebacker from the then new Super Bowl Champion Chicago Bears, entered the club. They were accompanied by a bodyguard, and caused quite a stir.

The Cotton Club is an intimate place, so where I was standing put me in close proximity to view Michael and Wilbur. The club arranged a private area of the bar for them, while allowing a few choice club regulars an opportunity to occasionally mingle with the superstars. I noticed two of the young ladies who didn't have time for any of us, the regular guys in the club. Somehow, they managed to get through the security to actually sit at the bar with Michael and Wilbur.

I thought to myself, how insincere those two ladies are to jump in Jordan's face, knowing if he was a regular guy they wouldn't say a word to him. Michael Jordan has said in interviews that before his fame and fortune, it was hard for him to get a girl to even look at him.

Now they were so frantic and excited, you would have thought they'd just won the lottery. After a while, I had done enough stargazing and decided to try my hand at asking someone else to dance. Being a little humbled by my first experience, I asked one of the heavier and lonelier-looking ladies, assuring I wouldn't get turned down for another dance. As I escorted her to the dance floor, I noticed no other couples got up to dance. We danced alone until, finally, another couple joined us on the floor. That other dance couple happened to be Michael Jordan and one of the ladies from the bar.

As the music played, Michael's huge bodyguard made his way to the dance floor, too. Because we were the only two couples on the dance floor, I danced over toward Michael Jordan, joking, while his bodyguard stepped closer making sure I gave Michael his space.

What made it interesting was that Michael and I had the same dance moves. Even Michael couldn't help but smile, noticing our similar style. That's not saying much, considering Donna has always teased me, saying I can't dance. But I'm quick to remind her that I dance like the greatest athlete of the twentieth century, so it can't be all bad.

At the end of the dance, Michael showed that infectious smile and shook my hand as others began piling unto the floor for the next dance. As he and Wilbur got ready to leave the club, the bodyguard told them the limousine was waiting. Michael and Wilbur proceeded to the front door, as people began grabbing for a piece of Michael. The two young ladies got up as if they were leaving with them. Michael whispered something to his bodyguard and the bodyguard turned to the young ladies and stuck his arm between Michael Jordan and them, as if to say, "Don't think you're about to go on a free ride."

I must admit, like every other guy, I felt vindicated to see those ladies pushed aside publicly. After the limousine left, I felt even more vindicated to see that no one asked them to dance for the rest of the evening. The moral of this story is Michael has the self- education that taught him how to survive in this world by dealing with others and knowing the difference between sincerity and social climbers. He is unstoppable as a person because he knows when to move away from the wrong crowd. Michael has proven over and over in his illustrious career that he is where he's supposed to be because he passed the test. There is a quote that says "Go not where the path may lead, but find your own path."

Not many of us can say we met the world's greatest athlete, and even fewer people can actually say they shared the same dance floor with Michael Jordan and learned a valuable lesson at the same time.

Preach Points:
- Formal education and self-education can make you unstoppable
- Don't try to take a free ride
- Learn to dance with greatness

4. Take Total Responsibility for Your Life

"The price of greatness is responsibility."
-Winston Churchill-

Practice What You Preach

<u>The inner journey</u>

Based on movies from Hollywood, one could believe that a knight on a white horse could come and magically take the princess away from all of life's disappointments and setbacks. But in reality, instead of wanting or waiting for someone to come along to fix the wrongs in your life, there are some things you can do for yourself before anyone else gets involved. First, you must have the *right attitude*, because attitude is 80% of what you will need to succeed. A *good attitude* keeps you in a positive state of mind. Your attitude is the way you think, act, talk and walk. Your attitude is something other people can actually see. It attracts success, and others want to share in it. The opposite is true for negative attitudes. Negative attitudes take more energy away from you. They can suck the fun and energy right out of the room. Attitudes play a part in your entire life, every minute, every hour, every day. So remember, you get out of life what your attitude puts into it.

After developing a strong positive attitude, make a committed effort to improve your own situation. You can do that by constantly changing and adjusting your life experiences and circumstances for the best results. Remember, it's not that you will be without tough times or misfortunes. It is how you approach and handle these times that will be the true measure of your journey. That effort requires you to take up an attitude that says, "If it is to be, it is up to me." That puts the onus on you first, looking to others simply as a support system.

Try not to take on other's problems, because, with your consent, it makes it very easy for them to simply dump their dirty load in your lap to wash. Then, when that load is not washed or handled the way they preferred it, you become the source of their perceived problem or blame. Thus, the adage "misery loves company" comes into play. You can't fill those voids missing in their life and they can't fill voids missing in your life. Don't set yourself up as anyone's savior, with them expecting you to solve their otherwise miserable situation. This becomes an impossible task, leaving you a permanent loser.

Even when you have a good experience, by not taking responsibility for your actions you can still be left in a bad fix. There are plenty of people who have wealth and don't take full responsibility for their actions. Over the years, scores of athletes, performers and people of influence have lost everything because they didn't take full responsibility for their actions, losing their fortune, faltering in their career and even going to jail. This leaves you and me baffled, wondering how people with so much could put themselves in a situation to lose it all.

Television sometimes portrays the evil rich person, who uses his servants or employees to do his dirty work. In these scenarios, the rich character shows a clear inability to be compassionate and hides behind his power. The same hiding is portrayed with the evil big boss who allows her employees to take the fall for her wrong actions. Both of these scenarios have the person in power arbitrarily irresponsible

Responsibility is misunderstood or misused in relationships more than anywhere else. You may ask, "Isn't the reason for a relationship for you to have your mate supply you with peace, love and happiness?" The answer is no, because no one person can supply you with inner peace, love and happiness: but God. The only thing your mate or significant other can do is share in the peace, love and happiness you already have for yourself, and vice versa.

Many marriages or relationships end because of a phenomenon known as *superficial dependency*, where one mate is looking for the other to take the responsibility to keep them both happy and satisfied. Usually, the relationship becomes filled with problems because the pressure put on the one partner is too unrealistic to maintain. Early in our relationship, Donna constantly explained to me that she was not a clown ready to entertain me when I walked in the door from work. It was my responsibility to have my own form of hobbies and entertainment.

Metaphorically speaking, you have to come to the dinner party bringing something to the table, and not just your appetite. In other words, you have to come with a dish in hand, or contribute to at least cleaning up after dinner. Because coming to eat at the table with nothing can lead to you eating alone one day and wondering why. That's a sign of being self-serving and self-centered. No relationship can survive that, unless one person is willing to sacrifice his or her own needs, leading a miserable existence, secretly looking for escape.

Ask yourself: "Can I put time and effort into something, believe it will work out and not selfishly take out?" You might say that every time you've tried to put something into the pot, others took advantage of you, leaving you hurt. This is where your faith in the law of "what comes around, goes around" comes in. The law states that whatever you put into life will somehow come back. So, it's still your responsibility to do the right things, regardless of what you think others might do to you, or the outcome.

This may be hard to swallow because your own limited beliefs can start to kick in, sending a signal of neediness, complaining, arguing, fighting or even procrastinating. Again, remember the most difficult thing to do is to go inside yourself and become the source of your own solution. Most of us will want to take an easy way out, and leave the situation in someone else's hands.

I would like you to continue on the road of Practicing What You Preach by understanding the principle of taking responsibility for your life. Taking responsibility occurs when you have claimed total ownership of your actions. To carry this out, you have to practice constantly changing and adjusting your habits, instead of supporting your weakest side. That means you can't give in to those things that have made you a slave to your circumstances; always make yourself stronger, not weaker.

For instance, I liked the company I worked for; it was one of the most prestigious and well-respected companies in the world. Though I disliked my manager's style, I continued to have a positive approach to my work ethics and my customer base; I tried not to give in to the negative environment he was producing. I also continued to find creative ways to let people know what I was trying to do as a speaker and writer. I had two speaking opportunities under my belt, with one good experience and one bad. Now I was determined to take full responsibility and make the next opportunity a success. I needed to create another speaking engagement. The opportunity came on a Friday evening, as I ended my regular sales day. I stopped by one of the major hotels to use a pay phone. Usually, I would check my voice messages, then make that one hour-drive home. Although this hotel was located in a predominantly white community, I noticed a large number of African American families checking into the hotel. Curiously, I walked over to one of the families and asked what type of event was being held. A lady responded, "We're having people in from all over the country for our family reunion." I asked her when were they having their family recognition dinner. She said the dinner was later that night.

This is where my desire to speak kicked in. I asked her if I could know who was scheduled to be the guest speaker. She said her aunt was going to say a few words at dinner. I asked, as if I were shocked, "You don't have a keynote speaker?" She looked confused, as I explained to her the latest trend in family reunions was to have outside speakers come in and talk about family values. I expressed my interest in speaking at her family's dinner, and asked her to introduce me to the family committee for their approval. I shared so much enthusiasm with them, that they decided to let me speak. I stayed around the hotel for a few hours rehearsing before my opportunity to speak.

I did my speech, and the family gave me a standing ovation. Several people walked up to me afterwards, and stuffed fifty-dollar bills in my shirt pocket. That reinforced my belief that public speaking was indeed a special privilege. You could say that was my first paid speaking engagement. I thought this was quite remarkable: These people had never seen me before, but I had become the guest speaker for their family reunion. I felt I'd taken responsibility of my destiny. I had changed and adjusted my skills on each engagement, assuring that I would progress and get better.   In my first three speaking engagements, I saw the good, the bad, and the ugly. I wouldn't stop here, because I had a chance to taste my dream, and loved it.   I had taken responsibility, along with   supporting my strongest self, and it paid off.

Preach points:
- Take responsibility for your life
- Become the source of your own solution
- Support your strongest self

Facts about writing a book

Reality kept reminding me that I had chosen two of the more difficult crafts: writing and public speaking. In my research, I found that fear of public speaking is one of the greatest fears among most Americans. The fear of speaking was ranked on one list as greater than the fear of dying. That information fascinated me, because I thought that if I mastered public speaking, the high risk would make the rewards even higher. I realized that public speaking is one of the most difficult, but most rewarding careers imaginable. It has giving me an opportunity to articulate my thoughts and help others improve.

Writing was no easier. However, the more I researched, the more enchanted I also became with that industry. It is reported that over   500,000 manuscripts are submitted each year in

America in the hope of being published. Out of the 500,000 submitted, only 55,000 are accepted for publication. Therefore, the majority of people never see their manuscript become a book. Sadly, it also says 445,000 people go without their dream being fulfilled. The more I read and heard about the publishing business, the more I realized I had to be one of the authors that would get my book published. I went back, refocused on my plan to spend time writing after work, while simultaneously learning and trying to speak on weekends.

Time will pass you by: Stop blaming

If you don't take responsibility for what you want to accomplish, fear can set in. *Fear can stop you in your tracks*, making you *stagnate about your goals*. That happened to me, during the period I began actually working on the book. Since I had written a few pages, the honey-moon ended. The question became, "how" would I write an entire manuscript, when I'm driving most of the time.

I decided to use a tape recorder in my car while driving to my sales calls. However, after several near accidents and a lot of bad taping, I realized that wasn't the best method for me. I couldn't type, so that was out of the question. Bottom line: I needed to get the information out of my head and on paper. Technology had become a big fear, even though Donna has always worked in the computer industry. It wouldn't have bothered me a bit if someone had said computers are now outdated and have become obsolete. Knowing that wasn't going to happen, I had to make a decision on how to achieve this lofty dream of writing a manuscript. The words of that wealthy real-estate man kept ringing in my mind: "If you were serious, the words would flow from your pen as though it were music to your ears." Several things helped me during that time that might also help you.

• Don't be afraid of technology: Find the best way you can work.

• Start somewhere. Most of us put off what we can do by constantly thinking about what we don't have.

• Be prepared once you backslide: Have motivators in position to lift you up when you fall.

Reality set in as I realized there is a lot of hard work in front of me. The bottom line was that I had to find a way to get over the fear. I also had to stop letting what I didn't know about the writing industry stop me from doing what I needed to do. One night, I sat in my office and put a yellow notepad in front of me. I sat there for an hour, before I started writing about the night my friend Garry "Deke" Kennedy was murdered. The next night, I wrote about the day I met my childhood friend Ray Grandberry. One page became ten pages, and then that became a hundred. I began to write regularly after work and on weekends. There were still times when I began to make excuses and procrastinate. Donna would often remind me about writing a book. I'd groan and pick up the notepads and begin writing again.

> "Always rise to the challenge
> of being challenged."
> -E. J. "Edge" Bassette-

Grinding it out

As the pages of those yellow notepads began to fill, I became more excited about seeing the words on paper. The notepads began to add up. I became obsessed with writing. I had those notepads wherever I went, including picnics, family reunions and even family Christmas parties.

I was always preaching to my eight older sisters and brothers about this book I was writing. Dad would look at me, shaking his head as though I had totally lost my mind. After two years of writing, I had written over 1000 pages. Finally, I thought, I'm done.

It's not over: Forgive and forget

During those two years, I was extremely encouraged with writing, and at the same time, I tried everything I could to improve my job.[8] I could see the *paradox*: everything I was building to achieve outside my job seemed so close, yet many things were being taken away from me in my job. I understood that all my efforts only meant something if I completed the task I set out to accomplish. On the other hand, because my job was draining me by this time, it was difficult to see the fortune or future. I knew I had fallen out of favor with management, and I was the target for a major fall. Each time my manager worked with me, he had some unfounded concerns. I found it difficult to separate myself from the situation, as I continued to take things personally and lose even more confidence. That lead to denial, and letting the situation dictate who I was instead of finding outlets for my frustration. Every time something happened, I let that anger build up and cause a range of negative emotions. The frustration continued to progress as I began waking up at night in cold sweats. I was not sleeping well, and I was constantly agitated. I'm not proud of it, but I was really stressed out about my situation.

This was especially true on days I had to work with my manager. The weeks leading to those workdays were some of the most stressful I can remember. After those days, I would come home from work and take out my anger on the family

8 Read "Silent Cry", part III. By E.J. Bassette

dog. The children could sense those times of anger, as they frantically tried to hide the dog. I would put my briefcase down and look through the house for him, as the kids begged me to leave their dog alone. I knew my work situation had taken over and consumed my personal, professional and family life. At the time, I didn't know how to master the fear and frustration I felt. Something would have to change, or, as Donna would say half jokingly, I would have to get a new address.

By the way, one night at dinner the kids had a vote on whom they wanted to stay-the dog or me. And you know whom they chose. Their buddy, the dog.

<u>Preach Points:</u>
•Don't take things personally: Learn how to keep from personally attacking your feelings about yourself. You can do this by separating who you are and what you stand for from what others say about you.

• Separate your family from your job: Don't define yourself by what you do. Keep your focus on your family and friends in the proper perspective.

<u>Look for a brighter day</u>

Because I continued to write throughout the difficult times in corporate, I finished those 1,000 pages of notes. I breathed a sign of relief, because I figured I had finally finished. Now I needed to go to the next step. Donna explained to me that the notes on the yellow note pads still needed to be transferred onto the computer. So I said, "Here they are; let's get it done." I figured she could type well so it would take about two weeks for her to complete all 1,000 pages. Donna assured me that between the children, homework, housework and the small computer business she was running, it would take her approximately two years. I couldn't believe it, as I sat holding my notepads cradled in my arms, wanting to cry.

> There is no future in any job. The future lies in the
> man who holds the job.
> -George Crane-

<u>Keep pressing forward</u>

For those two years of writing, I stopped trying to do public speaking. I decided to try to approach my corporate situation from a different perspective. I tried to pursue other positions in and out of my manager's area and in the corporate training field. All of those opportunities hit a stall and didn't progress past the initial stages. I didn't think I could possibly endure any more setbacks, as I searched for a reason why everything had to be so extremely difficult.

I started to search the local colleges, looking for a typist. One of my sisters, Eldora, lost her job. I asked her if she could type while she looked for a new position.

Donna also introduced me to a friend of hers, Wendy White, who wanted to make some extra money while attending college. So, Eldora and Wendy typed out my notes and everything began to fall in place-or so I thought. Midway through their typing, I anxiously started reading over the typed manuscript. Much of what I read was a different story line than the one they were supposed to type. They never informed me that my handwriting was difficult to read. So they both admitted to changing the manuscript to sound and read much better their way.

I couldn't believe this was happening. I sat up at night redoing each page in the manuscript. Typing with two fingers, I was determined to get the book completed. I had to continue to take and accept total responsibility for each phase of this project. I learned some valuable lessons that I would like to share with you.

Preach Points:
- Don't stop during tough times: If you stop, your dream stops . Regardless of how difficult it is, keep taking small steps toward completing your dream.
- Expect setbacks in a large project: Don't let every setback be a reason to quit. Understand and plan on setbacks. That will allow you to continue on without being flustered.
- Determination always wins: Remember, you are in it for the long term. So slow and steady improvement is better than quick and fast burnout.

> "To practice what you preach, you have to duplicate those things successful people are already doing"
> -E. J. "Edge" Bassette-

Don't be too busy to count your blessings

Like me, many of us can get so busy with the day-to-day issues and drama of our lives that we lose focus on what's important. We forget that we are magnificent gifts from God, put here to carry out His will and plan. He sends others into our lives to help us complete our mission. We all need others to believe in what we are doing. After you've received the help, you must stay on the path and acknowledge who put you where you are. In order to win God's way, you must become students of learning. You have to understand how to get the best results from the skills and knowledge you've obtained to this point in your life.

Most of us have unbelievable talents and gifts, but don't know how to use them. The talents go undiscovered, even though they are already right in our own back yard. We even go so far as to spend time wishing we had others talents, not realizing that the ones we have could be even more potent and powerful if we just knew how to use them.

This brings to mind a story of an African man who searched for diamonds his whole life. He was so consumed by his search for diamonds that he purchased land that was said to have diamonds on it. He moved his family to the land and worked it from morning until night, looking for diamonds. His obsession led him to neglect his wife and children. Years of hard work turned up nothing but huge rocks that lay under the surface of the ground.

Eventually running out of money, he and his wife and family were forced to leave. Out of desperation, he finally sold the land for virtually nothing; then, in a desperate act, he threw himself into the river and drowned. The new owner purchased the land for farming. But like the man before him, he discovered the land was full of huge rocks. Instead of throwing the rocks out, he studied them and found that once they were cleaned, they possessed a bright glare. The man discovered that these large rocks, once polished, were indeed diamonds.

The first man, who had the goal of finding diamonds, never understood that a diamond is rough until it's polished to get its luster and glare. It's one thing to have talent and dreams, but it takes polishing that talent to allow the true luster of the dream to show. You and I have to shine ourselves up to see the diamond we have inside of us.

Preach Points:
- Don't forget where your help comes from
- Understand the knowledge you have obtained
- Get the best results with the skill you have

5. Create a Personal Mission Statement-Your Dream List and Goals

"Brilliant people talk about ideas; average people talk about things; small people talk about other people."

-Unknown-

Understand the meaning of success

By Practicing what you've learned and Preached, your success rests on duplicating the universal rule that says you get out of life what you put in it. By using successful tools and strategies, overachievers have learned the keys to their success comes from their own ability to find out what they want and how to get it in a proactive way to further their results.

When they don't know about a particular subject or task, they make it a point to find out more information and become enthusiastically interested in knowing how to make things work. Instead of sitting back and letting those things that they don't know present greater setbacks, they seek more *wisdom* and *skill* in their endeavors, until they are able to master the problem. They subscribe to the old computer saying: "Garbage in, garbage out." Coupling their desire for mastering with a positive outlook and confidence puts them in situations to become experts in their field. This success makes it easier for them to visualize their goals over a long period of time, thus giving them staying power to hang in longer than others.

Because I had been exposed to these tools and strategies in corporate America, sales and college athletics, it allowed me a range of experiences and wisdom to operate with during difficult times. Although I didn't always want to experience the pain, I saw clearly enough to complete the first phase of writing my manuscript. I was continually drawing from the experiences I had learned all my life up to that point.

I knew I had become the number one sales rep in the nation because of acquired skills and abilities. No one could get to the top 10 percent of any profession without possessing certain skills such as a strong work ethic, clear mission, goals and a purpose.

Practice Points:
- Success rests in finding what you do and don't know
- Master your problems
- Gain staying power over a long period of time

"Success seems to be connected with action.
Successful men keep moving. They make mistakes,
but they don't quit."
-Conrad Hilton-

Equation for success

Proper tools are vital, because without them, you can't do the job. For instance, you can't put a nail into the wall without a hammer. You need the right tool to complete the job. The same is true for success. In order to achieve it, you must have the right tools. I have discussed success up to this point without giving the official definition of the word. Success, according to Webster's dictionary, is "a favorable result, the gaining of wealth, fame, etc." In other words, success becomes a relative term, whose definition is as unique as the individual seeking the success. For some, it's a nice family, or wealth, or good health. But whatever it is, there's one fact for certain: success should be maximized to its fullest potential. It is your responsibility to make success a priority in your life if you want to truly practice what you preach. Below is an equation that defines success and illustrates the importance of having the proper tools to maximize success.

This first equation says there are two key ingredients that make up success. Because success is different for each person, these key ingredients are particularly important. The first ingredient to success consists of having a vision. The key question is, Why? Without dreams and hope, there are only darkness and despair. So you must have things in front of you to look forward to, or your mind will start to die.

The second ingredient, which needs to be added to vision to complete the equation is action and constant motion toward your goals. Action, combined with vision, equals the results called success. So the equation for success looks like this: *Vision + Action =Success.*

Let's see what the success equation would be with one of the factors missing. V*ision + No Action* = Fantasy. This is a dream with no way to get it done. A lot of talk-with no action behind it-simply equals a fantasy. It becomes the world's biggest wish or fairy tale.

Another scenario is *No Vision + Action = Frustration.* For example, have you ever seen a friend continue to change methods of making extra money every time you see them? One day they're selling one thing, then a few months later they have totally abandoned that idea for a new one. That leads to confusion and frustration. Successful people have perfected the success formula; they now have the ability to stay with one idea over a long period of time and see it through to the end, making it work.

For other people, success eludes them because they never take the time to figure what it is that they want, or what personal success ultimately means to them. When you have started to work on your values and principles, you stopped blaming others and accepted total responsibility for your life. You have implemented the success strategy to find what is ultimately important to you.

Here are some other measures of finding success.

• Find something you love to do: If you find your love, you'll never "work" a day in your life.

• Have something that comes naturally: Continue to look for that gift that you do or have naturally. Ask friends and family what they see in you to help you develop those gifts.

• Experiencing a special feeling: When it gives you something special, you are more likely to pass the feeling of joy to someone else.

• Find what gives you an unfair competitive advantage: What comes easy to you but is difficult for others. Why would someone want to use you over a competitor?

Keep in mind, the measure of success is as different as the individual who is defining it, but the equations for success stays the same. For some, it's money, for others, it's power and for others it's family. I want you to take the time to define your personal success. For the sake of time, I want to keep it involved with your personal success. We will work with other successes later in the book.

I feel successful when I _____.
My success is _____.
Doing this gives me a chance to experience a special feeling of

_____.

You must put your thoughts in writing, because putting it down crystallizes the points and makes them official.

Over "the edge" dream list

Now that we have a meaning for success, let's start working on incorporating our visions into a personal dream. Let's develop a big picture list of all the things you're looking forward to accomplishing or obtaining. Ask yourself, what is it *I really want and why do I want it*? Remember, your dreams are important because they are what you hope for and aspire to. Earlier in the book, I talked about the little boy who wanted to be everything. Well, that little boy wasn't afraid to dream and use his imagination to think of unlimited possibilities. I really want you to go out there in this exercise. Note: Where there is no dream, the only thing left is a nightmare. Nobody can stop you from dreaming. You have to work on your dreams every available moment every single day. You have to live it, sleep it, and believe it.

I want you to write down everything you want to accomplish and things you want to achieve and places you want to go. Don't hold back, list all of them below.

"See it, Believe it, Achieve it"

_____
_____
_____
_____
_____
_____
_____

Before I started writing my first book, I read the book *Wealth without Risk* by Charles Givens. He instructed his readers to write out their dreams. He said one would be amazed at how many things on that list one would accomplish if one made it visible. One thing I had on my list was to write a book. Two years later, I had the makings of a manuscript. By keeping that dream list, I was beginning to change my life. I want you to write down everything. Go back over it and make sure you put everything down. Your dream list should shoot for the moon, so if you fall short, you'll still land among the stars. By writing your list out, you help clarify what you want. This allows you to go back over the information and update it at anytime.

"Some men see things as they are and say 'Why?'
I dream things that never were,
and say, 'Why not?'"
-George Bernard Shaw-

It's never too late to capture your dreams

Once your dreams are aligned with your mission, again you become *unstoppable*. No matter how long it takes or how difficult it is, you'll be able to handle the task. A true testament to this phenomenon is my sister, Evette, the youngest girl and the eighth sibling, out of nine. She can attest that most dreams take years of hard work to accomplish. Her dream started back when she was a little girl growing up in the Ida B. Wells housing development. Back then, she was very shy and reserved, unlike me. The one thing that stayed consistent was her dream to become a nurse when she grew up. I can still remember her talking about becoming a nurse. For as long as I can remember, that was the one dream she desired. When we were little kids, she'd pretend to play nurse on me, sticking me with one of her pretend needles.

By high school, she began working after school as a student nurse for a local hospital. I would often visit the hospital, and she would proudly introduce me to her friends. It was always a joy to see the passion she shared for her job.

Within a one-week span during June of 1977, Evette did three significant things that changed her life. She celebrated her eighteenth birthday, graduated from high school, and got married all in the same week. Within a year, she and her new husband purchased a building in a changing neighborhood on the far South Side of Chicago. At the same time, Evette started working on her dream by entering her first year of college to start the nursing program.

After a year of school, her husband suggested that she put off college to start a family. She agreed, and they had their first child. On hot summer days while her husband worked, she would sit with her baby boy on the front porch. Her husband suggested to her not to sit on the porch because he was concerned the neighborhood wasn't the best and didn't want young men looking at her or knowing she was alone. Then he advised her not to wear shorts or short sleeve shirts when she left the house, because he didn't want those same people to get the wrong idea. After a while he asked her not to leave the house, when he wasn't home.

While all these rules were slowly accumulating, their family grew, adding two girls. Though she loved her children dearly,

106

she began feeling isolated, as her self-esteem started to erode. At the same time, her husband's work slowed down, preventing them from acquiring many day-to-day necessities.

Over the years, the neighborhood changed into a drug and gang infested community. She grew more miserable, which often led to family squabbles. She was without a car or money- or her own dreams.

I would, along with other family members, often try to convince her to go back to school. I reminded her that she could be broke and miserable without all the aggravation. I finally figured a way for her to get some money in her pocket. Twice a week, I asked her to come over and help Donna and me clean our first apartment. She used the money as a way to provide some little things for her children. Evette walked her children to school every morning, protecting them from the drugs and violence of the community. Finally, Evette decided to donate time at the school so she could be involved in her children's education.

Spending time at the school helped her confidence come back. Being around professionals helped her see her value. The principal was aware of a parent-teachers program that allowed her to earn a little money. After putting up with ten years of lost dreams, verbal put- downs and low self-esteem within her marriage, Evette decided to go back to college and finish the three remaining years in the nursing program. Once she started night school, her husband did everything he could to stop her. He refused to baby sit for his own children and claimed she was an unfit mother. His disapproval of Evette's new-found confidence grew as she continued college; she often thought about dropping out.

For nine long years Evette struggled, cried, worried and often left her children at our older sister's and brother-in-law's house, Eldora and Robert, to finish night school. Twenty years almost to the day from the time I first saw her in that green nurse's uniform in high school, I'm proud to say my sister once again did three significant things in her life in the month of

June, 1997. Evette celebrated her 38th birthday, she graduated from a major university with a four-year nursing degree and she finally got a divorce. Evette started working at a local hospital and purchased her first new home. She's was able to move her children into a better neighborhood. Evette shared with those close to her, a quality that few people possess. She tapped into her ability to believe in a dream, and she refused to let go, even in the worst of circumstances. She ultimately stayed true to what she believed. For twenty years she didn't let go, and was able to change her life. Your dreams can change your life too.

(Evette became ill and passed away in October, 1999. Her hard work and sacrifice did not go in vain. To honor her, our family will start a scholarship in her name for young ladies who exemplify the courage and desire to live their dreams.)[9]

Practice Points:
- Follow your dreams
- Don't waste time
- Stay true to yourself

"A man without a purpose is like
a ship without a rudder."
-Thomas Carlyle-

Understanding your mission

Now you have a tight grip on what success is and what role it plays in your life. By writing out your dream list, you have put yourself in the right position for the next set of tools you'll need. You now need help to drive the success vehicle in the

---

[9] Check website for more information on scholarship www.3Binc.com

right direction. You're ready to understand your mission, or your ultimate purpose for being, doing and acting the way you do. Your mission is the "why" of your life. Your mission is not separate from the way you treat people or your *core beliefs*.

You've been evolving into the purpose of your mission your whole life. Without it, you feel lost, misguided and even cheated. It is said that there are only two reasons we are alive. One is to serve God, and the other is to find your mission. Your mission and your dreams represent two large parts to your life's puzzle. It's important to know there are smaller pieces, but the big picture has to be captured. Small day-to-day problems will always be around, but "Don't sweat the small stuff."

By seeing the whole picture or mission, you can begin to prioritize the big pieces of the puzzle. What I mean by looking at the big picture of your life is to not be hampered by the day-to-day details of your life.

To help make this point, I'll paraphrase an example, *First Things First,* by Stephen Covey. A professor placed some large rocks in a jar. Afterward, he asked, "Is this jar filled up to the top?" Naturally, the students answered yes. The teacher then took some small pebbles and poured them into the jar, as they fell between the cracks. He again asked the same question. This time, the students answered, "Definitely yes." So the teacher finally poured sand into the jar, watching it go between the large rocks and the pebbles. As the students looked perplexed, the teacher explained, "If you don't put your big rocks in the jar first, they would have never fit after you put in the pebbles and the sand. Those big rocks represent the big picture, and things you must accomplish. The pebbles and sand represent the smaller day-to-day issues and fires you must always deal with.

<u>Practice Points:</u>
• Without a mission, you can feel misguided

- Your mission is not separate from your core beliefs
- Your mission is the big picture

"Being a visionary is
to look beyond what you see and
concentrate on what could be."
-E.J. "Edge" Bassette-

<u>What is your life strategy statement ? Why write it out?</u>

A strategy statement explains your mission with a well-defined purpose, using your life, business or personal ambitions as a blueprint. A strategy statement gives you your mission in writing. By expressing your strategy statement, you are ultimately designing a lifestyle.

Think of the importance of the mission and strategy statement this way: A multi-million dollar company with hundreds of employees has to have a single purpose. The whole company has to act as one entity in order to carry out its ultimate goal. You can only imagine what chaos would occur if all those people were acting independently. The mission and strategy statement is crucial to that business.

The same is true for us to have the level of consistency in our personal lives. We have to have a mission and strategy statement to conquer that which is within. I like to call it the single voice of truth that drowns out the other struggles or voices distracting us from our true mission. Challenge yourself to have a strategy statement that will make you accountable for the goals you want to accomplish. When your mind is not used to getting you ahead, it becomes lazy and useless in your mission. Remember that at any given moment your subconscious is having a conversation with you, and more often than not that subconscious is telling you what you can't do. By writing out your strategy statement and keeping it in front of you, it will remind you of what you're trying to achieve. Also, by writing the statement out, it becomes a commitment to follow. Once your strategy statement is complete your purpose, principles, and desired outcome in a sentence, paragraph or an entire page.

-Your personal strategy statement should emphasize the following things about your mission:

-What I want to achieve with my life: What I'm I trying to do and how am I trying to do it?

-What my talents and capabilities are: What do I do best?

-How others will benefit from my achievement: How can I share my gifts with others so they can grow by my positive involvement?

-What I'm going to do: What exactly is my destiny? What is my passion?

-When I'm going to do it: What is my time frame to work on that destiny?

-How I'm going to do it: What are the means I will use to reach my destiny?

Write your strategy statement below. (Revise it every two years to update your mission.)

_____

_____

_____

_____

Now that you have stated your mission using a strategy statement, we have to find out how to make your dreams more focused.

"A winner is someone who sets his goals, commits himself to those goals, and then pursues his goals, with the ability given him."
-unknown-

111

Why Goals?

After you have developed your dream list, identified your personal mission and written the strategy statement that defines your mission, you have become a visionary. Embrace your own life and recognize the power you possess. Then, your power has to continue to be harnessed if your dreams are to become a reality. Your dreams are still the big picture, and you have to be detailed about each dream to make it accomplishable. You are a multidimensional being with many events going on in many areas of your life. It is vital that each area has its set of events taken from your dream list and prioritized into goals. The definition of goal is "An objective, a desired result or purpose toward which one is working."

Your goals have to be specific, individualized and personalized. For example, on a team each person has to know their individual goals, as well as the team goals. A perfect illustration of a team that had individual goals along with a single team goal was the series of six World Championship Bulls teams of the 90's. Each player had to know his individual position purpose and role. Within those individual players, you saw them winning scoring titles and rebounding titles, and making the All Star team; the team goal was to win championships.

Some people wonder: "Are goals necessary?" Without them, you run the risk of not staying on track. A train with no track has nowhere to go. This often happens when we don't understand the importance of time. There are plenty of people staying busy, but how many are truly accomplishing the things they want in a consistent manner? The fact is that less than 5 percent of the population has specific goals. That means a lot of people leave their lives to chance. Only 3 percent write down their goals, leaving too much room for error and goals not being met.

Here's a small illustration of why it is important to write things down. Have you ever gone to the grocery store without taking a grocery list? Isn't it almost certain you'll forget some of the items you need? Reports have also confirmed you'll always spend more money, because you're shopping more from a whim, than a written list. That's the same effect you'll have without written goals. You'll go through life wasting more of your time than needed. Here are some reasons you need to write down your goals:

• Helps you commit daily to doing them: You are able to review them daily, not forgetting what is important for you to accomplish.

• Makes you accountable to them: By having them in writing, you can measure whether you have followed through. This allows you to give yourself daily feedback.

• Allows you to focus and plan: By having them, you can plan and add new goals along the way.

Here's a goal-setting exercise that will help you determine and focus on your goals. Don't read any further until you complete it.

List each goal individually and fill in all the answers for each one.

1. Goal: _____.
2. I will start work on this goal _____.
3. I will measure my progress by _____.
(What gets measured gets managed. What gets rewarded gets repeated.)
4. What things stand between me and this goal_____
_____.
5.What benefits will result? _____.
6.What are the consequences of not finishing this goal
_____.

Break your goals into three categories: Short-range, medium-range and long-range. A short-range goal is immediately to six months; a medium-range goal is six months to a year; and long-range is one year and longer. Learn to do a little bit a lot instead of a lot a little bit. This process can also make your goals fun and attainable.

1. What are my short-range goals_____.
2. What are my medium-range goals_____.
3. What are my long-range goals_____.

Writing your goals requires a great deal of action, as well as vision. While writing them, imagine your own future five, ten or even fifteen years away. Reassure yourself that you will be doing better. Visualize your living quarters, family life and driving pleasures. What type of foods will you eat and how will you spend your days? What impact will you be making on this world? What forces will be trying to hold you back? As your goals become more visible, keep developing and reinvesting in your passions by reading inspiring books and listening to positive tapes.

Have fun in going after your goals and passions even if some of the them seem boring. Find ways to make your task inspiring by giving it all you've got.

Fear of failure and disappointment can stop you from trying. Continually ask yourself how bad do I want to accomplish my goal? Don't mind the wait because the longer the wait, the greater the reward.

"Ask yourself,
Would you take a test first, and then go home and study? That is same logic you use by not setting goals then living your life."
- E. J. "Edge" Bassette-

Momma's baby boy, Les Brown: The motivator

My speech at the family reunion had turned out to be a success, netting me some financial reward. My passion for speaking became even stronger. I knew speaking was going to be one of the vehicles I utilized to fulfill my dreams. My fourth speaking engagement, the one after the family reunion speech, also had positive results, leaving the college students ready for action. Afterward, a student said that I reminded her of a great motivational speaker named Les Brown. I was not aware of him until I became familiar with his brilliant seminars on PBS.

Les Brown is a world-renowned public speaker, who has been acclaimed nationally and internationally as one of the top five public speakers in the world. He is a self-made millionaire, and one of the country's most popular African Americans. A friend of mine named Percy "Tookie" Tompkins[10] invited me to see Les Brown.

Les Brown was speaking at Christ Universal Temple, which has one of the country's largest congregations, is located on the far South Side of Chicago. I was so excited that I invited my brother, Eddie and others in the family to attend. As I sat in that audience of more than 4,000 people, feeling the electricity in the air, Les Brown's words and style helped reassure me that public speaking was the best profession in the world. He was the first very successful African American man I had ever seen doing what I envisioned doing. That day left me with a thoroughly positive impression of Les Brown and the public speaking industry.

I truly believe there are people willing to assist you in whatever you are trying to accomplish in life. I also believe you can ask or look for the wrong support from others if your goals and intentions are blurry. I had such an experience while attending the Les Brown Speaking For a Living Workshop

---

10 Read "Silent Cry" Part III. By E.J. Bassette

given in Chicago. I signed up for a three-day workshop to learn more about the speaking industry. As the first day of the workshop approached, I decided to change my goal and take it upon myself to make Les Brown my personal mentor.

Two hundred people attended the first day of the workshop. As I scanned the room, I saw Les Brown nearby. I became star struck as I watched him walk around, mingling and laughing with everyone. I decided at that moment he was going to be one of my best friends too. After all, I was a successful businessperson and now an aspiring speaker and author. Why wouldn't Les take me under his wing?

I walked up to Les and introduced myself, thinking this would kick off a long conversation. He politely spoke and complimented me on my attire, then turned back around to finish his previous conversation. A little stunned, I figured I still had time. I set my goal to be his star pupil. Then over time, he'd be sharing the speakers' platform with me around the country.

By the end of the first day, Les Brown had become familiar with a number of people and none were named E. J. Bassette. I called home to Donna, discouraged and disappointed, saying "Honey, I don't like Mr. Brown anymore." "Why not?" she asked, after listening to me intently. I exclaimed through the phone in an animated voice, "Les Brown ain't all that nice. Plus, he's arrogant anyway." Pausing for a moment, I then said, "He won't even spend time with me." Donna asked in a loving voice, "E. J., are you there to kiss Les Brown's you-know-what, or are you there to learn about the speaking business from the workshop?" To say the least, I told her she didn't understand and hurried off the phone.

The second day, I tried the same strategy, and again it didn't work. I wasn't any closer to Les Brown. For the second day, I called home complaining to Donna, this time telling her that I now *hated* Les Brown, as well as hated the workshop. For the second day, Donna listened to me, and again asked me what was my purpose for being there. She encouraged me to refocus my goals and expectations and to learn the speaking business. Donna asked a question that helped me see the light. "E. J.," she asked, "What have you learned about the speaking business, and who else in the organization have you met?" I was so focused on being Les Brown's friend, I hadn't honestly learned much of anything. I promised her I would change my intentions.

The last day of the workshop, instead of focusing on Les Brown's friendship, I decided to learn as much as possible. I also met all of Les Brown's support staff. They were all very approachable, helpful and very easy to talk to. His staff also shared vital input about the speaking business that I needed to know to get started.

I gained such valuable information from the staff, I decided to stay in touch and build relationships with some key people after they returned to their home office in Detroit. I volunteered to help out whenever Les Brown came into Chicago to speak. I offered to assist in the sale of his book and tape products after his speeches.

Several months later, a staff member took me up on my offer. I showed up at the event early, and to my surprise, Les Brown was already there. I had an opportunity to sit down and talk with him uninterrupted. Later in the evening, his fiancée at the time, the legendary Gladys Knight, sang. After selling his products, I was allowed in the dressing room, which gave me a chance to meet her.

I learned how Les prepared for his speeches before he went on stage. I also learned a lot about how to sell books and tapes at major events. Later in the evening, Les and Gladys headed for the door and I offered to carry his case. Picture this, Les Brown, Gladys Knight and I walking to the limousine. Les held his hand out to assist Gladys into the limousine before getting in himself. Then I stuck my head in and Les laughed at me and said politely, "Your day is coming."

The moral of this story is that though I truly believe there are people in the world willing to assist you in what you want to accomplish, it may not happen the way you expect. Also be clear about what your goals are. Unrealistic goals produce blurry and unrealistic results. My initial goal failed: I wasn't his best friend or star pupil. The key is that I adjusted my goal. Make your goals realistic, then regroup and try again. Use plan B if plan A doesn't work. When your goals don't work, refocus and keep going.

By the way, one of his staff members turned out be his daughter, Ona Brown. We have since become good friends. She is also a speaker and a trainer based in Chicago and Florida, and she has recently authored her first book.

Preach Points:
- Intentions have to be crystal clear
- Ask for specific help from others
- Articulate what you are looking for before asking
- Keep goals realistic

Everything you want to know is in a book

I read books by famous speakers, trainers and motivators, some of their books where very helpful in my development: Les Brown's *Live your Dreams* and *It's Not Over Until You Win.*, Brian Tracy's, *Psychology of Achievement* and *100 Absolutely Unbreakable Laws of Business Success*, Anthony Robbins' *Awaken the Giant Within*, Stephen Covey's *7 Habits of Highly Effective People*, Dennis Kimbro's *Think and Grow Rich*, Stedman Graham's *You Can Make It Happen* and Dale Carnegie's *How to Win Friends and Influence People*, and Tony Alessandra's *The Platinum Rule*. I realized all the information I needed was put in books and on tapes.

I had to do some more research to get more information. I also decided to get involved with some of the organizations they recommended: the National Speakers Association-Illinois Chapter, Toastmasters International, Meeting Professionals

International, Convention Management Association, National Sales Network, Chicagoland Chamber of Commerce, Southland Chamber of Commerce.

As I attended these organizations' meetings, I found many of the speakers and trainers there, like Willie Jolley, Jim Meisenheimer, Michael Wynne, Frank Bucaro, John Blumberg, Mark Sanders, Deb Gauldin and many others. I found some of the speakers had written and published their own books and tapes series. They were publishing their own products and selling them in the back of their seminars. These people as well as others, such as John Watson, John Erby, Diane L. Gregory, David Richardson, Nile Gossett, Sue Tinnish, Michele C. Wierzgac and Jessica Boykin and the organizations they represent became a wealth of information that still spearhead my development as a writer and speaker.

What types of books do you need to read for your development?

1._____.
2._____.
3._____.

What organizations do you need to join?

1._____.
2._____.
3._____.

Preach Points:
- Readers are leaders
- Everything you want to know is in a book
- Join organizations

6. Seek Out a Balanced Life

"Ask, and it shall be given you; Seek and ye shall find..."
Matthew 7:7-8

The Ten Principles

<u>Where to start</u>

Let's stop here and review the first five principles to Practicing What You Preach. Remember, each principle is designed to assist you in taking more responsibility for your own success. You also make a better quality of life for yourself. When these five principles are practiced together, they give you an inside track on using all of your potential. The five principles are:

1. Start where you are today.
2. Develop your philosophy and ideas.
3. Operate out of your values and principles.
4. Take responsibility for your life.
5. Write a personal mission statement, outlining a dream list and goals.

While practicing these five principles, your *state of mind* becomes more confident and aware that you are headed in a more meaningful and purposeful direction. You have organized your plan and written out your goals, thus putting the script for success right in front of you. Again, the first five principles are *personal steps*, because all the growth has to come from your own desire. I contend that if you are not unleashing all of your abilities, then you're not giving yourself the greatest chance for success. This sixth principle pulls the first five principles together by adding balance.

Now it's time to add the sixth and final principle that has you working independently and making changes from within, not having intervention from others. This sixth principle has to first be developed within you and become self-motivating. After you are self-motivated, then you can receive assistance from others.

The sixth step deals with *seeking a balance*. The balance I'm discussing is designed to give you the quality of life you desire on all levels. The balance will be broken into six categories; each one will be discussed in detail in this chapter.

You may ask, "Why is it so critical to have balance, when do you have it and how do you achieve it?" The "why" about balance is important when you deal with the age-old questions of harmony, stability and equilibrium bringing about success and happiness.

If you believe that everything in the universe has a place, then one of the laws of nature says that everything in the universe directly or indirectly depends on everything else. So, all of your conscious and unconscious states of mind play an important part in the good of the whole, therefore sharing a distinct purpose. Since you are part in the universe would it be safe to say your actions play an important part of the universe? Yes. The same is true for every living creature and thing. They all play a part in the consistency of the universe. You need everything and everything needs you.

Just as the world and all its organisms have a designed purpose, you, too have a profound purpose. They seek their purpose by doing the job they were placed here to do. For instance, trees, birds, insects and rivers run in natural cycles, fulfilling their purpose and playing distinct roles in the overall good and balance of the world's eco-system.

You can fulfill your purpose by seeking the balance that is required and becomes essential in your life. Because human lives are complicated and filled with choices and decisions, balance is more difficult to achieve than imagined. That's why you have to make the proper choices to find the natural balance. By finding the choices, you are putting your life in harmony with your Creator because you are holding in front of yourself, the often overlooked big picture of life.

Remember, the big picture of your life needs to operate with all the subtotals equaling the whole. Once all the parts of your life are connected, they bring a more productive, fulfilled life.

In sports, it's easy to get this point of balance across. Recall when Michael Jordan was in the earlier part of his basketball career. Everybody acknowledged that he had great individual talent. The one negative knock on Michael Jordan initially was that he didn't display a *complete* or *balanced* basketball game. The media often made references to him as not being able to make the players around him better. So as Michael Jordan matured, he become more balanced, being aware of other parts of his basketball game other than scoring. Giving more attention to the balance improved the overall ability of the team, and the Chicago Bulls won six championships. For that, Michael Jordan went into history as the most complete all-around basketball player ever to play the game- and as perhaps the greatest athlete of the twentieth century.

As an equation, balance is defined as giving energy to the big picture, plus maximum output. That equals success which is higher productivity plus completeness of ideas plus total happiness. It is both balance and success that are essential to the quality of life you are seeking. In final equation form it looks like this: *Balance (big picture + maximum output) = Success (higher productivity + completeness of ideas + total happiness)*

Although success for each person is different, depending on your needs, desires and wants, we all know that each individual has free will, choice and a paradigm which has been created and based on their own reality. But to achieve balance, you need to achieve all your abilities.

It's easy to achieve in one area of your life while letting the others decay. That can make you content with the level of accomplishment you've achieved, while making you a candidate of underachieving. Another example might say that based on your reality, you are perfectly content ignoring your loved ones in your pursuit of success. That can leave you feeling very successful in one area, while feeling like a complete failure in another. In corporate America, I find a number of high-level executives to be business geniuses, able to motivate hundreds of employees, but they are terrible parents, not able to relate to their own children. Doctors are often saving other's lives, but are letting their own personal relationships die. By having balance and seeing the big picture and giving maximum output, you don't have to go through life denying yourself of the pleasure of living your life while operating on all cylinders. By making the choice to develop all the areas, you give yourself the ability to appreciate your talents, with a clear conscience, leaving no regrets or concerns. That makes your life complete, productive and happy.

Recall the third principle, which teaches you *happiness is in existence* when things you *believe* in are *consistent* with the things you *do* on a *daily* basis, or H= B+C+D+D. You need a belief system that says a balanced, healthier life style is better for your personal life as well as your professional life.

In accounting, a balance sheet shares with you an update as to how all the money is accounted. That accounting sheet also shares the value of your account. Your life balance sheet is the same, sharing the value of your life, and how you affect the lives of others. Steven Covey, the author of 7 *Habits of Highly Effective People*, says it perfectly, "People don't care how much you know until they know how much you care."

In order to reach a high quality of life, you will have to stretch yourself beyond the boundaries you've stretched consciously before. That means you won't get until you give, and for some of you that means coming out of your comfort zone. That might mean you have to leave the office early and take your kid to the movies or spend some quality time with your spouse or significant other.

There are six areas of balance you will have to practice to be consistent. Balancing these areas may turn you 180 degrees from your past. Once you share the responsibility of taking on these priorities, you will see that your overall wellness depends on your balance.

Preach Points:
- The laws of life bring a full and complete life cycle
- Wellness depends on your balance

- Balance (big picture + maximum output) = Success (higher productivity + completeness of ideas + total happiness)

<u>Operating in the zone</u>

The six areas of life in which to achieve balance are your family, spiritual, financial, intellectual, social and mental/physical/emotional lives. These areas must be fulfilled to obtain an ultimate quality of life, bringing true and total success. Remember, as discussed before, people often choose one area to excel in, while ignoring the other areas totally. For example, some people are misguided in thinking of success only in terms of financial wealth. So they pursue happiness with the sole purpose to obtain more possessions. But buyers beware: even the most material people eventually find their emotional bank emptied, while searching for that elusive "happiness" they desire-never acknowledging that without a strong proactive spiritual life, physical health, family or friends to share the wealth with, money and things have little value. To be a well-rounded person is paramount, and balance is the ultimate factor needed.

What does it truly mean to live your life completely in balance? I equate it to what athletes call the zone. Metaphorically, the zone is a state of consciousness that athletes are in when they feel they are doing everything right on the playing field. During interviews, you often hear of basketball players expressing that theory when they say the basketball hoop seemed as big as an ocean. In other words, they could do no wrong. They seemed to be able to see everything in slow motion, while playing the perfect game.

In athletics, the zone is the highest level of conscious and subconscious achievement. A person in that zone is like watching a man playing among boys. You can achieve that same effect and feeling of having your life operate on a higher consciousness, where all the things you are experiencing come together. Your life is taken to another level from those operating around you because you are now displaying some of the positive attributes of a true champion. These attributes have to be displayed constantly to live your life in the zone. Mike Ward, one of the managers and mentors I enjoyed in my corporate sales career, calls these attributes *C.A.D.-Fire*. With the combination of these attributes, you can be unstoppable.

- **C**: Commitment
- **A**: Attitude
- **D**: Desire

- **F**: Focus
- **I**: Interest
- **R**: Results
- **E**: Encouragement

With the combination of these attributes, you become the person others pattern themselves after. You live your life in the family, spiritual, financial, intellectual, social, mental/physical/emotional zones.

Preach Points:
- Six areas of balance
- "The zone" is a state of consciousness
- Balance is where all the things you work for come together.

"Some people want to enjoy the fruits of their labor while others enjoy passing out their fruit so others can eat."
-E.J. "Edge" Bassette-

The Ten Principles

Family Balance:

A family contains the most important *structure* known to mankind. Family means just that. A group that is related to each other. This unit has to have each other to depend on, learn from and nurture. Family units elevate their lifestyles and existence through developing better and more efficient ways of sustaining their lives. Humans are not the only group that supports family. It is seen in all of the animals. Just open your window on a spring morning to hear the sounds of baby birds asking for their breakfast. The same is true for mammals rearing their young to hunt, guaranteeing their species a means to survive.

Unfortunately, with the advancement of human society, we have forfeited our families to look for this elusive objective called success. This success becomes so vague that we make excuses to obtain it while leaving the very relationships we need and love. It is not uncommon to hear about a man who leaves his wife and children after the wife has spent her best years caring for him. While he studied in medical school, she worked long hours to make ends meet and to care for the children. But upon graduation, reaching a time to reap the shared benefits, he says, "Thanks but no thanks." He becomes obsessed with his job while losing the purpose of taking care of the family who took care of him.

By becoming so obsessed with his job, and so self-centered and selfish, he can lose the fact that raising a family to maturity is a natural law of the universe, with all the blessings attached. The other paths disguised as "success," can bring about a sense of failure and indifference.

Your life has to be centered around sharing the success and joy you obtained with the family who helped you along the way. You do this by getting your family involved with what is going on in your life. You have to trust the people closest to you by letting them share in your happiness and your pain.

Practice What You Preach

Family means doing things together, like having dinner hour or watching a movie. Raising children is a full-time job, all day every day. A few days ago, my ten-year old daughter, Niki asked me if I was a taxi driver. She says I spend a lot of time driving her and her brother and sister around. In order for them to be involved in their activities, Donna and I have to be involved with them. Most importantly, the fact that children learn from having structure and discipline. Without that structure, they float through life learning the wrong messages from the wrong people. As a kid , one of my fondest memories was seeing Dad drive up and park the car after work. Even though I grew up in the Ida B. Wells projects, Dad was and still is the most positive influential role model in my life. With him as a mentor, came the belief and comfort that everything could work out all right.

On the other hand, with the divorce rate being over 60%, fewer fathers are living with their children. The scene for many young people is that of not having male influences at all. That emptiness stays with our youth, making them more susceptible to gangs, drugs, violence and poor grades in school. Studies show that a balance of family leaves children secure, and gives them a better outlook on life and success.

People who have overcome great obstacles develop a great insight on the importance of balance and family. Recently, while working out in a local health club, I overheard an older gentleman talking to his friends about life and balance. He expressed to his buddies how he had successfully fought and won the battle against colon cancer. I eavesdropped to hear the story about his ordeal. He related to them how money had come and gone, and the thing that helped him during his time of need was the strong relationships with his family. Although he was financially wealthy, he realized his real wealth came from the lives he touched and the grandchildren he was leaving here to carry on his legacy.

I'm very proud of the work Donna and I have done with our children. Deanna is in high school, Mario is in eighth grade and Niki is in fourth grade. They all are lovable children.

Take a moment, to answer these questions about family.
1. My family is important because_____.
2. My family helps me to accomplish_____.
3. Want to help my family accomplish_____.

Preach Points:
- Family contains the most important structure known to humankind
- Success becomes so vague that we make excuses
- Family means doing things together

Spiritual Balance

We need to know that our true strength is not in our physical bodies and not driven by flesh but by *spirit*. We often get caught up in the day-to-day grind of this world and all of its trappings, and we forget that God has a greater destiny for us than we can ever imagine for ourselves. We get overconfident in taking the credit for ourselves and lose the very power we are trying to receive. As human beings, we have to know our strength comes from God, and He is the source of our being. Alone, we can't accomplish much, but with God, all things are possible.

Knowing that with Him if *all things are possible*, you shouldn't get beside yourself when good things happen. The Bible teaches that "As long as we seek the Lord, God will make us prosper" (2 Chronicles 26:5). So expect to be empowered as you keep God as your source. His force and power will be the center of your love, joy and happiness.

You build spiritual strength through prayer. Prayer becomes the food that keeps you fed with His word. Build that strength when things are going well. By constantly reading the Bible and other spiritual references, you are able to build up your spiritual muscle as an athlete builds up his or her body, preparing for a particular sport. If you have no spiritual muscles, then you have no defense toward the opponents you are facing.

Also, build up your children by teaching them how to reach out for God's love and mercy. When I was a little boy growing up, every morning Momma prayed with us as a family. Now as a man, I pray with Donna and our children every morning before we all go our separate ways. The Bible teaches, "The just man walketh in his integrity: his children are blessed after him" (Proverbs 20:7). Remember, don't you leave prayer, and prayer won't leave you.

Even when you fail, God loves you enough to stay by your side. Don't complain if you haven't done what you need to do. Pray for the strength and guidance to go against that which makes you weak . Do the work and plant the seed before you start expecting a harvest.

You and I must maintain our mental peace of mind. Keep seeking and finding your beliefs by surrounding yourself with people who are spiritually and morally grounded. Spend time reading, studying and reflecting on the words of God for yourself.

1. I know God is in my life because_____.
2. I need to get stronger spiritually because_____.
3. I will teach God's mercy to my children because_____.

Preach Points:
- With God, all things are possible
- Build spiritual strength through prayer
- Know God for yourself

Financial Balance

Your financial well-being is crucial to keeping overall balance in your life. When your financial profile is healthy, it gives you the *leverage and freedom* to do what you need and make the choices you want at the time that is appropriate. In other words, you won't be a financial slave to your boss, job , lifestyle, credit cards or any other crutch. A poor financial situation often stops many people from fulfilling many of their dreams. More often than not, money, or lack of financial support, is a leading concern, stripping most people of their option of taking advantage of an opportunity. To keep your financial picture healthy, I have a few rules, that, if applied, can make a huge impact: 1. Have a family budget. Always know exactly what money needs to go out and exactly what is coming in. 2. Live below your means. Live off a portion of your salary, not your whole salary. Don't live paycheck to paycheck. 3. Don't let credit cards and interest ruin your finances. By living below your means and budgeting, you should have an excellent grasp on your bills. You have to focus on your needs, not your wants. Don't try to keep up with the Joneses. 4. Always save at least ten percent of your earnings. This guarantees you to pay yourself first. Plan up front for that rainy day. 5. Plan for your complete long-term success by always staying abreast of what's going on in the financial arena. Learn about mutual funds and stocks, as well as real-estate and other financial ventures. Make an appointment with a financial analyst, someone you trust to help you with your portfolio. What you have to remember is the fact that financial success is not how much you earn. It's how much you keep. Your net worth is key.

Once you become financially balanced, your options in life will begin to open, giving you more freedom and making you feel more empowered. Remember, don't strictly view your overall success in terms of how many material purchases you can make. You still need the other five elements of balance to lead a healthy lifestyle.

1. My financial goals include_____.

- Have a family budget
- Live below your means
- Don't let credit cards ruin your finances
- Always save at least 10 percent of your earnings
- Plan for your complete long-term success

Intellectual Balance

Your intellectual thirst for knowledge has to be maintained. Your knowledge is rooted in a need to know and a need to grow. There is a saying that *readers are leaders*. One of the wealthiest woman in America, talk show host Oprah Winfrey, says that even though she grew up poor, reading books gave her the opportunity to travel around the world without leaving her small poverty-stricken hometown. Yes, she traveled around the world, using the power of her imagination. Then, through hard work and determination, she took advantage of different opportunities. Her experiences from those books manifested themselves into real dreams. She, along with thousands of Americans, has learned this secret.

Consider developing your *intellect as a passion* and an investment in yourself. By going deep into the vast wealth of knowledge available, you can truly turn knowledge into power. On the other hand, ignorance is the worst plague on any person or society. Ignorance robs you of your self-esteem and dreams, causing all types of breakdowns and problems. You see it every day in the large school systems across the country, where some schools have a 50-percent dropout rate. That leaves generations of young people illiterate and handicapped, without the option of a better future.

Knowledge is everywhere you look. Using the Internet, libraries, bookstores, and schools, you can become an expert in any field of endeavor by practicing the principle of *intellectual stimulus*. Humankind has been capitalizing on its intellect since the beginning of time-but like everything else, it has to be balanced with other areas of influence to bring true success.

List 5 books you want to read:
1._____.
2._____.
3._____.
4._____.
5._____.

Preach Points:
- Readers are leaders
- Need to know and a need to grow
- A person can become an expert in any field of endeavor

"You have to take care of others first, if you want them to take care of you."
E.J. "Edge" Bassette

Social Balance

Social balance is the art of *developing relationships*. This is one of the more difficult skills to attain. Most of us are caught in times of need with no person, support system or information to turn to for help. This means it is imperative that you keep healthy relationships with good friends and family who support what you're trying to accomplish. You should be able to call the right person depending upon the need. You should be in a position to leverage your good deeds with the people you have established relationships. Alliances should be built through networking and acts of kindness.

Your relationships should be widespread and far-reaching. Author Harvey Mackay wrote *How to Swim With the Sharks Without Being Eaten Alive* and *Dig Your Well Before You're Thirsty.* In these books, he gives hundreds of how-to's in the areas of networking and relationship building effectively. Harvey makes a point to share with his readers what the ideal circumstance would be to make friends before you need them.

Right now, you may socialize within a small circle, not recognizing the need for having other friends and associates. You may feel the limitations of this small circle when you find yourself in a circumstance of needing advice, perhaps from a lawyer, doctor or mechanic. Just when you need someone you can trust, you find there is no one by your side.

You should network with people at your job, in case you find yourself on the outside looking in. Not knowing someone is no reason not to network. Have you heard the saying, "A stranger is a friend you haven't met yet." With that, as a motto, you are sure to increase your network. Without it, when a time of need arises, you have no one but yourself to blame for never reaching out. Here are some tips for socializing:

• Bring value into any friendship or relationship: Start helping others, without asking for anything in return.

• Sincerely doing nice things from your heart-unconditionally- is the best place to start.

• You must help others for them to help you: Find people in your sphere who give you the trust and honesty you need.

• Separate yourself from people capable of bringing you down with pity parties. Don't allow those people to fester around you, interfering with your dreams-or even causing you to give them up.

Three people I need in my circle:

1.

2.

3.

Preach Points:
- You need good friends and family who support what you are trying to accomplish
- Most of us are caught in a situation with little or no information about our subject
- Avoid people who bring you down with pity parties

Mental/physical/emotional Balance

It's hard to reach optimal success when you are lacking the mental, physical and emotional well-being you need to carry out your dreams. When I was younger, I would often hear the older people say, "I may not have much, but I'm blessed because at least, I have my health." I didn't appreciate what they were saying until I became an adult and realized that without your health, it's almost impossible to accomplish your dreams.

Without mental and emotional strength, it becomes difficult to focus on the task, at hand. Without your physical health, you lack the energy and stamina it takes to keep your dreams energized and moving forward.

Let me share some ways you can keep yourself physically and emotionally balanced. The first way is to eat a proper diet. The saying "you are what you eat" is true. To be proactive about what you put into your body will pay dividends down the road to a longer and healthier life. Try eating more *nutritious meals* by adding plenty of *fruits and vegetables* to your diet. A healthy diet can be the best medicine you can take in the long run. Also talk to your health care provider about the right vitamins and minerals your body may need to supplement your diet.

The second important aspect is to *exercise* on a regular basis. Your body is the most unique and complicated machine ever designed. It also has the capability to heal itself with the proper assistance from its landlord, you. But just like a computer, it has to be properly maintained in order to perform, or it will break down. The same thing will happen to your body, if it's not properly tuned up. Your body gets a tune-up when you allow it the proper rest and exercise to maintain a strong heart and bones. My Dad is a true testament to this because at 81 years old he still rides a bike, exercises and manages to maintain a high level of activity. I always say he is 81 years old, going on 31. He is a great inspiration for anyone who is seeking a long, productive life.

Talk to your health care provider about developing an exercise program for yourself. Also, get regular medical checkups to help yourself maintain the proper weight, blood pressure and other vital areas for a long healthy life.

A final aspect to good emotional balance is having a *positive outlook* on your life and the outcomes of your efforts. Remember: things will happen to you, but it's how you handle them that will make the difference in your overall health. Avoid allowing stress to build by counter acting in positive ways. Use relaxation techniques like meditation, prayer, yoga or a number of others to seek relief from the stress. Learn to proactively minimize the stress.

When you approach your life with a healthier outlook, you will be giving yourself a chance to be around to enjoy the fruit of your hard work and labor.

Preach Points:
- Eat a proper diet
- Exercise on a regular basis
- Have a positive outlook on your life and the outcomes of your efforts

The greatest skill

One of the greatest gifts you can give to yourself is the ability to improve and master your *life skills*. Improving your skill set will bring a better balance, taking you to that higher level of being and operating called "consciousness." What skill stands out as the most valuable one of all? The answer to that question is the *ability to communicate*. By communicating, humankind has been able to develop new frontiers, allowing different nations an opportunity to share, build and grow. On the other hand, without good communication, misunderstandings occur, walls are built up physically and mentally, and wars occur destroying the progress that has been made. Individuals who can communicate their ideas rise to the top of their profession. So remember, as with the entire world, communication in your life is the one skill needed to advance your six areas of balance.

Preach Points
  • Your ability to communicate is the greatest skill
  • Share, build and grow

Grade your improvement

After you've balanced your life, how do you keep your life headed in the direction you need it to go? The answer is to constantly *update and measure your progress* by keeping accurate *written accounts*. This process is important to track and upgrade your skills, by keeping the results and how you used them. There is a saying: "What get measured gets done." By measuring your progress or lack of progress, you are able to gauge the actual rate of growth. By constantly checking, you can know at a moment's notice if you're on target, or if you need to change the course. This system takes out the excuses and procrastination that can accompany your growth. Without measuring your skills or progress, you can delay your growth by years, or even a lifetime.

How do you grade yourself? One way to grade yourself is to ask others to monitor your improvement. This includes your toughest critics, like your spouse, children or parents. Ask them to monitor your level of communication. If you really want to be bold, ask others outside the family, including co-workers.

- How will success change or improve my life?
- What will I invest or trade for becoming successful?
- What does success really mean to me?

Preach Points:

- Measure your progress
- Track and upgrade your skills
- Monitor your level of communicating

7. Create and Build Lasting Relationships

"A single conversation across the table with a wise
man is worth a month's study of books."
-Chinese proverb-

Practice What You Preach

The importance of listening

"Each of us needs all of us" is a phrase I live by and believe in. That belief keeps me searching for the best of myself and others. It also keeps me open to talking and communicating well with others. People who truly practice what they preach tend to be the *best communicators* on the planet. They are also great *listeners* who stay connected to a circle of high achievers, leaving the majority of others on the outside looking in. Why is it they have this ability to associate with the best? To answer this question, you have to first look outside of yourself. Listeners love learning from others, and have a vital advantage in an area that most people lack: Listening as an art form. Most people think of communication as simply opening their mouths and telling all about themselves and what they want.

What do you think people like to talk about most? You're right-themselves. By letting others have the stage, you are making a connection for life. In actuality, what has to be mastered, communication-is the art of listening. Not talking, but listening. Listening is the most difficult skill to master because the attention is taking the focus off you and putting it on someone else. Listening 50 percent of the time should be the goal to having productive, meaningful conversations.

By using selective listening skills, you can build excellent relationships. By asking the right questions, you can make the conversation flow easier. By smiling, you invite others to share. By remembering to use a person's name, you personalize the conversation. Always let other people do more of talking. Intently, show interest with positive body language, and nodding your head in agreement.

Great listeners encourage others to talk about themselves, to share their strengths, joys and even disappointments. Always ask others about their interests, making them feel important. When responding to a question, give an honest and sincere answer, not criticizing or condemning the speaker. Let others feel the power of having an idea be theirs. Be empathetic with the other person's ideas and desires. Your growth comes from seeing things objectively from someone else's point of view. You will always develop friendships and associates easier by being proactive instead of reactive. By listening, you become proactive; you become empowered because others want to share and get your input.

To become a better listener, I must:

1._____.
2._____.
3._____.

Preach Points:
- Take your focus off yourself and put it on someone else
- Listen at least 50% of the time
- Encourage others to talk about their interests

Good of the human spirit

After you've listened, your human spirit still has to reach out to offer help to your fellow humans. For example, when huge disasters strike, people from all over the world rally together. Then during their normal day-to-day living, people tend to retreat into their isolated shells, not caring about their neighbors, friends or other fellow humans. This happens when people tend to disassociate themselves from others' experiences. This *disassociation* makes them look at others they don't know with indifference toward their misfortune.

Indifference is one of the most debilitating misfortunes you can bring into someone's life. Indifference says, "Because I don't know you, I don't care about you, or what you stand for." To take one's life's work for granted can be devastating. It goes against the human desire to be loved, noticed and cared about. People can find it hard to go out of their way for others because it causes them to feel vulnerable.

For us to truly develop our human spirit, we must take the attention away from ourselves and concentrate on others. Helping others, first doesn't come naturally, because most of us think of ourselves first.

Many of the great men and women we admire put the cause of other people before their own personal gain. That character is not always practiced, but is always admired. By doing this, you will get everything you ever wanted and more. Zig Ziglar, one of the greatest motivators of our time, says it perfectly. "By helping enough people get what they want in life, you'll get everything you want. Think about what situations would make you reach out to give to others. To grow into your full potential, you have to give until it hurts, then give some more while going out of your way to help."

Preach Points:
- Become a person who calls for action
- Great people put the cause of others before their own personal gain
- By helping others, you will get everything you ever wanted, and more

> "If you look hard enough, you'll find it: and if you work hard enough, you'll get it."
> -E.J. "Edge" Bassette-

Give until it hurts

I began meeting and networking with other speakers and writers, forcing my paradigm to continually expand. While reading a business magazine called, *Black Enterprise*, I read a cover story on a speaker and writer named George Fraser. He had recently written a book entitled *Success Runs in Our Race*. The article described George as the master of networking in the

African-American community. After reading this story, I was so excited that I wanted to contact him. I later found out he was coming to Chicago to promote his book at a business exposition.

At the expo, I visited his vendor's booth, and shared with him my vision about finishing my first book. I asked if he could share any information about how I could promote my upcoming book. Without hesitating, he said to call his office in Columbus, Ohio, the next Thursday. He offered to supply me with over 400 media contacts that he had built relationships with. I graciously thanked him and walked way, until I asked myself, how will he remember me out of all the hundreds of people he'll meet at the Expo?

I walked back to his booth, and voiced my concern. He assured me that if I called, he would get me the information I needed. Satisfied, I walked away again, thinking to myself, he's just saying that to blow me off, knowing he won't see me again.

So I came back to the booth again intending to expose him as a fraud. "Mr. Fraser," I asked, "why are you going to fax me all this information when you don't even know me?" He looked me in the eye as though I was the only person around and said, "You said you needed help and that's what I'm doing." So I asked, " Why would you help when so many others make a token gesture and never follow up?" He replied, "You give until it hurts, and then you give a little more."

That Thursday, I called Columbus and just as promised, those 400 media contacts came rolling off my fax machine. I understood his message to go out of your way and listen, to understand, then help others, not turning away. George gave me more than media contacts; he also gave me a model to follow.

Preach Points:
- Share your vision
- Ask for help
- Follow through

<u>What goes around comes around</u>

A few months later, I read in the local paper that Mr. Fraser would be doing a book signing at the historical DuSable Museum on the South Side of Chicago. By then, I had shared with Donna the story of how he was so supportive of me. I was excited to see him, and Donna wanted to hear him speak about his new book, *Success Runs in Our Race.* At the end of his lecture, I noticed people still debating whether to buy his book. Seeing this, I stood up with my baby daughter in my arms, Donna by my side, and explained to the audience how he helped me, a local Chicago author, to get started on my dream. Then I ended by saying I wanted to be the first person in line to buy his fabulous book. Those people almost knocked me down to get in line before me to buy his books. When I came around, he graciously thanked me for speaking so honestly about his actions and his book. I looked at him and said, "Give until it hurts, then give a little more." One day you may be able to give to people, when they least expect it.

1. What could you give until it hurts? _____.
2. Whom can you help and how?_____

_____

_____

_____

_____

_____

<u>*Preach Points:*</u>
  - Find ways to help others
  - Always be gracious

"Some men dream of worthy accomplishments,
while others stay awake and do them."
-unknown-

The cost of a dream/ behind every good man is a better woman

Donna and I had been saving a little nest egg for our kids' college funds, retirement and emergencies. Now, I was finding out that self publishing a book had a huge cost, including promotions, extensive research, brochures, mailers and other marketing tools. These costs, along with the cost of printing the books, would put the price in the thousands of dollars. When you have a dream, you must be aware that there is a cost that goes along with it.

For most people, dreams stop right there. The average American couple has less than $3,000 in savings, or about three months of living expenses. Because of poor planning up front, most dreams are cut short. Low cash flow to no cash flow can become our greatest enemy. Because Donna and I had planned for a rainy day, there was money available. Now I had to convince Donna to agree to use our life savings for this business venture.

So I sat with Donna, and showed her the plan, then asked her if could I borrow our family savings to get this book published. After I had many discussions with her and refined the plan, she agreed.

Publishing a book requires a lot of hard work. We had to outsource everything: The editor, the book cover, the printing and all the other hidden costs.

1. What is the industry in which your dream will be?____

_____.

2. How much will it cost to start your dream?_____.

Preach Points:
- There is a cost that goes along with your dream.
- Poor planning cuts most dreams short
- Work part-time on your dream. Get familiar with the industry research

> "Look for key to your door instead of breaking the door down first. Don't always look for the quickest answer."
> -E. J. "Edge" Bassette-

<u>You need angels around you</u>

I was spinning my wheels, not knowing where to turn for all the things I needed. Friends of friends directed me to a friend from college who had published two books. James immediately shared his contacts and referred me to his editor, cover designer and printing company. I know that without him, publishing a book would have taken me an additional year or two to find the right information and people to work with.

I entered different stages of trying to get the manuscript completed. I was advised to let people read it and give me constructive feedback. So I passed it out to friends and family who said they enjoyed reading. I asked them to highlight and critique areas that needed revising. But as time passed, I noticed most of them weren't returning my manuscript. Even my professional editor didn't realize the amount of work involved. Because everybody I had reading the manuscript fell further behind schedule, my spirits began to sink low because I didn't think I would ever get the book completed.

I learned valuable lessons from those experiences, like not to take it personally. Even though, I felt my back was against the wall, faith was all I had to rely on. I still knew that without my editor, my book wouldn't have been nearly as far along as it was at that point. This book had been in the making for over three years now. I had to become totally dependent on others' skills to complete their part of the agreement. I had no more to give, because I was emotionally drained and psychologically, a wreck.

I shared my dilemma with a lady who supervised one of my corporate accounts. Over the years, Carol had become a good

146

friend, and a few years earlier, I even volunteered to go into her son's high school to speak on Career Day. Now, Carol was returning the favor by offering to read the manuscript.

At this point, so many others had let me down, I really didn't know what to expect. After Carol received the manuscript, within a few days she called me and said she had read through it, corrected it a half dozen times. I was stunned, as she raved about how good the story line was. I couldn't believe what I was hearing, because I had spent so much time trying to get people to read the manuscript once. Carol read it, corrected it, offered suggestions and even asked if she could continue to work with me to see it into reality. Carol's support of my efforts became invaluable, as she helped me get over the finish line. My editor did jump back into the process at the end to help smooth out the content and subject matter.

When it was all said and done, between Carol, family, friends and the editor, the manuscript had been revised over 30 times. As a tribute to her, I asked if she would write a favorable response on the back cover. I can't say enough about having winners on your team-people who believe in what you're doing.

I'm sad to say Carol died of cancer in 1998. I'll always remember her friendship, and how she came to be an *angel* in my life. Carol's words will be forever remembered on the back of that book.

Preach Points:
- Don't let others get you down
- There is always someone near to help you
- Carol is a true angel

The squeaky wheel gets the oil

Once the manuscript was completed, Donna and I researched other books to get the exact font, cover and format we wanted. Donna carefully selected a printer after receiving bids from all over the country. I simultaneously worked on the front cover and the title of the book. I used pictures of Ray's son and my son on the cover, and I settled on the title *Silent Cry: Ray, Deke and Me, The Keys To Stopping the Violence.*

Once the printers received our manuscript, they were able to give us a target date for completion. But unforeseen printing delays caused them to put the book on hold. My book, although a fairly sizable job, couldn't compare to some of the huge printing jobs this printing company was used to doing. The book was being pushed to the back of the line, so that more lucrative jobs could be printed first.

Because I had financial commitments, I had a huge sense of urgency to get my books. The lesson I learned here was this: If you're going to see your dream through, be ready to fight for what is yours. Be ready to dig in for the long haul, because nobody else will fight for you.

I had given the printers my money up front. Now it was time for them to deliver the books. I had heard horror stories from small publishers trying to print their books for distribution. For example, one lady showed me the books her printer printed for her. He printed the books in the basement of his home. After she received her shipment, she noticed the ink was not sticking to the pages. The stitching that binds the cover and the pages together was coming apart. Finally, she found her printer selling the books to the bookstores himself. She had to laugh to keep from crying.

Preach Points:
    Be prepared to fight
    Fight for what's yours, because nobody else will

The dream finally came: thousands of books

There is a saying that most people drown three feet from the shore. They give up, not realizing that with a little more kick and effort they would be safe.

At this point, I felt like giving up. Then my middle brother, Eric, stepped in and said he would help get my books. Eric infused new life and energy into my cause. He decided to drive to the state where the books were being printed to let them know they couldn't continue to delay my book order. Eric said he would drive to the printing plant every day if necessary to show them that we were serious. Because the printing was so far behind schedule, I was losing money. I didn't have books to sell.

Eric and I made several visits to the printer's plant. Finally, they announced the books were ready. Eric and I rented a delivery truck and drove there to pick up the books. It was one of the proudest days of my life-walking into this huge, world-renowned printing company, and seeing my new book *"Silent Cry"* coming off the printing press. I could see my new company's name, 3B Motivation, Training & Development, on the side of these huge boxes of books as they were loaded on the rental truck. To see my dreams and hard work come together made me feel I had accomplished one of the greatest feats of my life.

My oldest brother Eddie's dream came true also. That same week, he and Joyce, his life partner, opened their first men's clothing store, *B-Elegant*, on the south side of Chicago. Later, my sister Elaine, purchased the hat shop called *Lourdes Hats*, right next door to the clothing store.

Practice What You Preach

Preach Points:
Let others infuse new life unto your cause
Don't drown three feet from the shore

Now the real job starts

As I mentioned earlier in this book, many couples plan for the wedding day, and not the marriage. They practically go into shock when the person they've married comes home to live with them. The vows say "in sickness and health, in good in times and bad, for richer or poorer." I instantly felt the same commitment of a marriage to these thousands of books I had ordered.

Now three long years had passed while writing and reliving the fun, joy and pain of the lives of Ray, Deke and myself. Some of the writing tore at the core of my soul. During the same three-year period, the job I had once loved and had mastered, became the job from hell. In many ways, writing had become a way for me to voice and channel my anger about my corporate nightmare. The payoff was that I had done what few thought I could accomplish.

I had written about the joys and pains, failures and successes of my life and the lives of others. I had written it and published it, and now I had thousands of books on my doorstep to prove it. Yes, thousands of books that I had picked up and brought home.

I was excited but overwhelmed with unloading hundreds of boxes, containing thousands of books. The boxes quickly filled our house. My children were jumping around, filled with excitement, as they saw boxes being stacked from the floor to the ceiling. I think they thought it was Christmas, but internally I wondered what I had gotten myself into.

Eddie's dream of having a clothing store had also became a reality. He had the similar challenges, stocking his store with hundreds of suits, ties, shirts and other clothing.

Preach Points:

- Channel your anger unto something productive
- Don't question your hard work and efforts

"Feed your faith, and your doubts will
starve to death"
-Unknown-

Don't look back

I had practiced what I preached by putting all our money where my mouth was. I had no choice now but to leave the safety net. I knew I had to leave corporate America, the place where my paycheck had come from for the past decade. I had to leave it behind to pursue my own path. Now was the moment of truth. Was I going to sit on the sideline and be a spectator, or was I going to get in the game? What did I have to lose? Why was I so afraid? Could I really get out there and speak for a living, and sell all these books? Was I going to follow the plan I had set for myself? All these questions were going over and over in my mind.

In one way, my job had already made it easy for me. Because of all the difficulties I was having, they had all but fired me by this point. But like some of you, even with all that chaos, I was still afraid to leave. Most of us stay in bad jobs, marriages and other relationships, long after they have caused us mental or psychological scars, afraid of what is unavoidable.

In my case, I confided with Donna and my mother-in-law, as they both assured me that going on with my life and leaving the past behind was better and healthier. I have to admit there are not too many mothers-in-law who will tell their sons-in-law to leave their job. Donna agreed, and admitted she'd rather see me leave such a stressful job, causing sleepless nights and frustration. It just wasn't worth it, and life is too short. I had to stop operating in the anger that my manager had made me feel. Anger can make you lose your focus and stifle productivity. You must find ways to manage that anger before it causes any further damage –to yourself or others.

A: Acting
N: Negative
G: Generating
E: Evil
R: Results

If that anger is used properly, it can be a force of energy directed positively to serve your ultimate purpose.

Preach Point:

  • What positive idea, action or attitude can you generate from your anger?

"People can alter their lives by
altering their attitudes."
-William James-

Role reversal

I decided to sit down with Donna and come to an agreement. I wanted to speak full-time for a living. That meant that for the time being, she would have to work full-time. I believe there has to be one *dreamer* and *one income* per family. But Donna had been out of the workforce for five years and didn't care for the corporate lifestyle.

Donna had already let me tie up all our money in printing the books. Now I had one more favor to ask. "Honey, would you consider going back into the workplace so that I could sell all these books we have in boxes filling up our house." Donna had a few concerns about the children. After all, they were the reason she stopped working in the first place. Her concerns were their day-to-day discipline, homework and after-school interaction with us. After hearing her concerns, I thought, like most men who leave for work in the morning and come back in the evening. If your only concern is the kids and all that stuff, how hard could it be for me to supply them with their needs? In the heat of the moment, I started assuring Donna of all of the things I would be available to do for the kids. I even added doing all the daily household chores. I promised Donna that every day I would be home by 3 o'clock when the kids got off the school bus. I would help them with their homework, clean the house, help cook and even do the laundry.

In other words, I would wear the apron. I knew it couldn't be that difficult, could it? I pleaded my case until she became comfortable enough to agree to go back to work. Finally, after long discussions she decided to give it a try. I was so excited I almost jumped through the roof.

But as time passed, Donna didn't seem as excited about actually looking for a job. I had gone ahead and given my resignation to my company. So as time passed, we were finding ourselves in a bit of a financial crunch because she was getting cold feet. One of us had to work because the bills would soon be piling up. I started to stress out because she was only half-heartedly pursuing job opportunities.

After questioning her, I found she had sent only one resume out for a job. As we argued, times became tense, but, before we could finish arguing, the phone rang from the company she had sent the resume. They were impressed with her qualifications, and requested a time to interview. I was so excited that I picked out her clothes and almost dressed her myself, pushing her out the door. She got the job.

<u>You get what you ask for</u>

Donna started working full-time, and I started speaking, and keeping to my original promise to be back home by 3 p.m. When Donna got home from work, I would be standing in the kitchen with that apron on. One day as she came in, while setting her briefcase down she noticed that I was leaning close to the stove, with my head down and my hands over my eyes. She came closer and noticed a few tears.

I looked at her and said, "You just don't understand. I just cleaned the house, and before you got home, these kids messed it up again." I explained to Donna how nice she had it, not doing homework and dealing with the day-to-day kid issues. Then I told her that she still expected me to have my hair done, looking cute for her. And all I hear is her complaints about her job. She knew I was totally overwhelmed with my new responsibilities, but she was quick to remind me that I got what I asked for.

Preach Points:
- You get what you ask for
- Don't make promises you can't keep
- Raising children is the toughest job in the world

<u>Go for what you know: My first sale</u>

After we unloaded all those books from the rental truck, I stuffed my duffle bag with 25 copies of *Silent Cry: Ray, Deke & Me: The Keys to Stopping the Violence*. I went out to my car and drove to the nearest gas station. I had to convince myself I could sell this book. I had been the number one salesman at a Fortune 500 company, and if I could sell for them, I could sell for myself.

I walked over to an older man pumping gas and held the book up. I explained to him that the picture on the front was me. He said he would purchase it if I agreed to sign my autograph. I was so nervous that I messed up his name. After that I began selling them on the street, door to door, in parking lots and even to parents at Chucky Cheese Restaurant for kids.

My career takes off

Soon after, I started speaking in schools, companies, churches and associations and other professional organizations. The book allowed me to gain exposure and credibility. My speeches were being accepted by people of all walks of life. I decided to go to the church where I saw Les Brown speak regularly, at Christ Universal Temple. As I met with Reverend Helen Carry, the youth minister, I expressed my interest in working closely with their youth. I had worked with a member of their church, Dr. Winston Johnson, an elementary school principal and tremendous speaker and mentor. He was nice enough to refer me to Reverend Carry and Dr. Johnnie Coleman.

Dr. Coleman had built the wonderful Christ Universal Temple complex, though many people had thought she was too old to pull it off. The complex has over 4,000 seats. Dr. Coleman has a national following, and she is very selective about who gets to stand at the podium and address her congregation.

Many great people had shared the podium over the years. The funeral of Harold Washington, the first African-American mayor of Chicago, was held there. Reverend Carry was impressed with my presentation, and gave me an opportunity to speak to the youth center that was off to the side of the main complex.

The teenagers enjoyed my speech, and a few months later Reverend Carry called me again to ask if I would speak for a Sunday service to the entire 4,000 member congregation.   As Reverend Carry discussed the details with me over the phone, I began to think back to when I told my friend Tookie that I would be speaking at that great podium one day. As Reverend Carry continued the conversation, she informed me that two speakers were being considered: the Reverend Jesse Jackson and "ME". That's when I began to shake nervously. She called me the next day and told me that Jesse would be their speaker for that Sunday. Before I could let out a sigh of relief, she said, "We decided to have you come the Sunday before him."

Preach Points:
- If you can do it for others then you can do it for yourself
- If people enjoy you they will refer you

Check your ego at the door

The speaking business took off quickly, and my ego started to get the best of me. I began selling hundreds of books, meeting literally thousands of people. I was being requested for interviews on television and radio and in newspapers. And I was speaking 20 to 30 times a month. People were waiting in line to buy my book and get my autograph. I often came home exhausted to a wife and three kids. Donna would constantly ask me to help around the house to keep my end of the agreement we had. One time as she spoke, I looked at her with a totally confused expression. Then I finally said, "Honey, you don't understand. People love me and wait in lines to have me autograph their books. I'm a celebrity now. When I come home, don't expect me to do housework."

Without missing a beat, Donna said, "You're so special in this house we want you to take out the garbage." Needless to say, I mumbled to myself and did as I was told. But it took a while to separate who I was, from what I do. Most of us struggle when we lose ourselves to ego and arrogance.

Preach Points:
- Don't lose yourself to arrogance
- Remember where you came from

The power of networking

I continued my training in the speaking industry by learning from other professional speakers. The National Speakers Association annual conference facilitates over 4,000 trainers, speakers and consultants from all over the world. Some of the biggest names in public speaking come to share their input. One year, the keynote speaker was Harvey Mackay, the author of the best-selling of *How to Swim with the Sharks Without Being Eaten Alive* and *Dig Your Well Before You're Thirsty*. He is a master networker, who has spoken in a Fortune 500 company at least once a week for over the past five years. He's also the president of Mackay Envelopes, which grosses millions of dollars a year.

After his keynote address, I asked him to take a picture with me. He was more than gracious, as his personality mirrored the same person he portrayed himself to be in his books and on his motivational tapes. He accepted my book, *Silent Cry* and asked me to call his office in a few days to get a copy of his latest tape set, compliments of him. I was on a high for weeks on end as Mr. Mackay made a friend for life. By practicing what he preached, he impressed me enough for me to write about him in my first book and this book.

1. Ask yourself, who would write about you?
2. Whom have you affected in a positive way that they think enough of you to share your story?

Preach Points:
- Learn from veterans in your industry
- Do you mirror the person you are?

"Don't settle for what you know, but for what you need and want to know in order to grow."

-E. J. "Edge" Bassette-

Winning with the big boys

Now that I was fully involved in the speaking industry, it was the knowledge and those experiences obtained in corporate America that kept me going. On the one hand, I knew that I had found my niche. I was gaining confidence in the speaking and training industry. Sure, there were still roadblocks along the way. But I had the big picture at hand. I knew that I could be focused while learning from the past. I was confident because I had done well before and now I could do it again.

In most instances, this public speaking business was no different than running a sales territory in corporate America. I had had many successes there, as well as many disappointments, but now that I was on my own, I had to learn from the mistakes and expand on the positive experiences. I would try to keep those positive experiences in the forefront of my mind, reminding me how much talent I really had. One positive experience I like to share is from my corporate days, something that happened after I read *How to Win Friends and Influence People.* (This book is a masterpiece on how to win and build relationships.)

At a major sales meeting, the president of our company shared the good news of his daughter having her first baby, who was his first grandchild. As all my peers let that information go in one ear and out the other, I made a note in my appointment book to call his secretary. I asked her to let me know when the baby was born. She followed up, and Donna and I picked out an outfit for the new grandson and sent it to the president's office with regards from our family. At the next major meeting, as the president arrived, people flocked to greet him. I was standing back, away from the crowd. However he noticed me, left the crowd and came over to shake my hand, expressing his gratitude for the present his grandson had received.

Later, before he began his presentation to the national sales group, a picture of his grandson wearing the outfit we purchased for him appeared on the huge telescreen. For the second time, he acknowledged me, in front of my peers, and publicly invited me to view more pictures of his grandson later. Most of my peers wondered how I created this relationship with the president. Why did I seem to get recognized, when they so desperately wanted it? Here are some keys to becoming irresistible:

- Go the extra mile: Always find ways to give more than you are getting in return. Learn to give when it's not expected.
- Share a professional intimacy: Share a part of yourself that says, "I'm willing to let my guard down."
- Don't burn bridges: find creative ways to work with people, always keeping the door open to come back.

Creating win-win relationships:

In order to win, you have to be able to create relationships that are beneficial to yourself and the other party. Whenever I've done a seminar for the residents of a Chicago housing development, I give them my full respect and attention. I don't save that respect only for corporate audiences or professional groups. I want you to question your actions with others because there are people who try to get by with being insincere, creating bad relationships, while ignoring and exploiting people.

Some people still make it to the top of their industry but still burn many bridges along the way. These relationships can be personal or customer related. For example, at one time, large department store chains didn't feel the need to operate stores in small towns with populations of 10,000 people or less.

These large chains were doing well in the industry without the small rural customers. By failing to listen, and build *win-win relationships* with *all* the potential customers and *markets*, large chains left themselves vulnerable to competitors. One of those competitors was a man who grew up in a rural area and understood the needs of rural customers. He decided to service customers with discounts in small towns, where the big-name chains ignored them. This man's name was Sam Walton, and the discount stores are called Wal-Mart.

By not building win-win relationships and not taking care of a need, even the number one chain slipped in market share, while Wal-Mart grew to become the number one retailer in the country. Just like Wal-Mart, you have a chance to build the relationships that bring you closer to your objective.

We are all in the *people/customer* business. Some of you just don't know it yet. Some of your best alliances will come by building strong win-win relationships. Don't go through your life burning bridges, creating enemies, wondering way you are not meeting your own expectations. Also beware of *toxic relationships* masked as true friendships that leave you in a worse state than before.

List five people you can build better relationships with.

1._____.
2._____.
3._____.

4._____.
5._____.

<u>*Preach Points:*</u>
- Create relationships that are beneficial
- Don't ignore the customers
- Don't burn bridges

<u>The ultimate win- win: For life</u>

My speaking opportunities were not limited to one particular market. I always made sure a part of my speaking efforts were back in the inner-city communities, where young men didn't see a lot of positive role models. I had a speaking engagement at a public school near the housing developments I had grown up in. I had already spoken to the students at the same school a month or so earlier. Now, I was invited back to speak at a teacher-parent meeting one evening. I was due to speak about 6:00 p.m. The sun had already gone down on this cold winter evening in Chicago. As I drove into the parking lot and collected my materials from the car, I noticed six or seven young men approaching me in the school parking lot.

Because the hoods from their coats were pulled so far over their heads, I couldn't see any faces. My first thought was that they would be up to no good and I would be the target. I figured I was in the wrong place at the wrong time. As they got closer, one of the young men shouted out, "What's up E. J? You want us to help you carry your books and stuff to the school?" You don't know the relief I felt because they recognized me from previously speaking at the school. I had already created a relationship with these young men that could be of help in their lives.

We say we want young people off the street, but how many of us actually share our gifts with them, making them better people? I had built the ultimate relationships. Instead of having young men wanting to rob me, I had them wanting to help me in my efforts. When you win the respect of young people, you are really doing something special. I now have that relationship with over 100,000 young people over the last few years.

The ultimate relationship-the one you want to strive for-is a *win- win relationship*, developed when both parties are getting something positive from the exchange. On the opposite side is a lose-lose relationship; when both parties lose from their exchange, that is considered a nonproductive, and even destructive, relationship. Other relationships, where one of the two parties loses, is authority driven. One person in the relationship is at a disadvantage, while the other receives the advantages.

How can you win when you keep losing?

You have to build good relationships with the knowledge that true friendships, marriages, business, and relationships are not tested when things are going well. When things are going badly is when the true test really comes. You expect people to feel good about a situation when they're making money, or they're in the honeymoon period of the relationship. But what about the grunt time, when things seem to be falling apart. That's when your true *commitment of character* comes out. How do you react when the business is not where you expected it to be?

The true commitment character of a team was demonstrated some years back when the world-championship Chicago Bulls were on pace to be the first NBA team in history to win 70 or more games in one season. Michael Jordan, already noted as the best basketball player in the world, had made a comeback from baseball and the tragic death of his dad. After returning with a disappointing playoff loss to the Orlando Magic, Michael had a lot to prove.

I'm a huge fan of Jordan and Scottie Pippen (they are responsible for my getting cable TV), and I loved seeing them win the 72 games in one season back in the nineties. But I paid particular attention to how they handled the 10 losses that year. You see, people expected them to win every game. So after each loss, the media magnified it, expecting a panic. But Jordan and Pippen always handled the questions with the best attitude, sharing their true *commitment of character*. Each time, they restated that their overall objective was to win a championship. They also addressed the need to analyze the film and practice the fundamentals to get back to the basics. Imagine that, Michael and Scottie wanting to practice and get back to the basics. Now they will go down in history for their efforts.

Preach Points:
- Make and keep a commitment to character
- Learn how to handle losses
- Get back to the basics

Keep going

I spent the first year three years speaking wherever I could. The honeymoon period had ended, as the initial rush of speaking engagements and book sales started to flatten out. I had hit the initial base of people. All my wonderful friends and family, who had been supportive early on, had settled back into their normal routines. Now, the speaking business was not going as smoothly. I was expanding my speaking and training opportunities into unfamiliar areas. The cash flow was getting tight as I started to rethink what I was doing and how I was doing it. To gain some confidence, I invited a friend to hear me speak at a corporate managers' association meeting.

I was thrown completely off-guard before the presentation, when I learned that my sponsor had changed the topic I was to speak on without my knowledge. I did the presentation the best

I could under the circumstances. But to make things worse, in an effort to give me constructive feedback, my friend blurted out every negative point he could about my presentation. He even told me I didn't fit the image of success because I didn't wear a thousand-dollar suit and drive up to the event in a limousine. I was hurt because he couldn't relate to my business. I explained to him I no longer had a corporate company car, unlike him. I drove a used car I had purchased from my brother, Eric.

I had taken a chance and started over from nothing, as I had done years earlier coming out of college and working with my oldest brother, Eddie. So once again, the car I drove had more rust on it, than gas in it. I had spent every ounce of time, money and energy to start this business. It was easy for my friend to talk. He still worked in corporate America which supplied him with a new company car, expense account and a nice salary.

He could not relate to my journey into the world of entrepreneurship. I came home that night and actually decided that I'd just quit. But after a few days, there was no one to answer the phone or take out the garbage because I was also the secretary and the janitor of my business. After a few more days of feeling sorry for myself, I dug deep into my *attitude bank* and my commitment to character. I had to avoid the anger and fear that comes along with the frustration.

Many of you feel the same way, under-appreciated and ready to give up. Just like the Bulls would do after a loss, I had to review what had gone well and figure out what could I improve on. Go back and practice, get on the phone and get back to basics. No, I wasn't riding in a limousine and I didn't have a thousand dollar-suit, but I was doing my best. I was a champion, because, unlike my friend, who could only see the downside, I had chosen my destiny and I was doing it my way. By the way, I did go to Eddie and let him dress me for success with his B Elegant Men clothing store. So we formed an alliance to work together once again.

Preach Points:
- Find friends who can relate to your journey
- Avoid the anger that comes along with frustration
- Dig deep into your attitude bank

Can you stand the pain?

"Why isn't your book in all the bookstores?" This is one of the questions I was constantly being asked. In our original plans, Donna and I decided to put books in all the bookstores around the country, while keeping a portion of books to sell directly to my speaking audiences. I talked to many authors and had gotten mixed feedback on what they had experienced with the book industry.

When dealing with bookstores, you have to go through distributors (the "middle-man"). There are approximately 5,000 bookstores in the country. Small publishers printing a first-run book have to be very careful as to how many books they are going to release in the market. Once those books are released, they become almost impossible to get back if they don't sell.

Then there are tremendous discounts the distributors expect, which range from 30% to as much as 70% off the list price of the books. Then, instead of paying for the books up front, they want the books on 90-day consignment. If the books are damaged or stolen, the distributor is not responsible. Many small press publishers have lost all of their investment because they got caught up in trying to grow too fast by having their book all over the country. Some of these stories made me leery about the book industry.

I did put my book in several community bookstores. When two of the stores went out of business and one moved, I never received my books or the money for them. I've had a hard time getting money from some people standing right in front of me. They have money in their hand and ask me if my book was in a book store. And my reply has been, "You're looking at the book store." Now I am on the national distributor list that allows a store to get my book off the Internet and order it instead of tying up my inventory. My book is also available at Amazon.com and Barnes and Noble.com.

Practice Points:
- Research the market
- Avoid a middleman if possiblc
- Explore using the Internet to market your business

Do you believe in yourself when others don't?

One night, Susan Taylor, publisher of *Essence* magazine, was in Chicago to promote her new book. She was giving a lecture on the South Side of Chicago. The owner of the bookstore that was sponsoring Susan asked me to come out and set up a booth to sell my book. By the time I got there, people had already formed a long line to meet Susan and to purchase her book. While she was signing books in one room, the audience in the auditorium was patiently waiting to hear Susan's presentation.

The owner asked if in the meanwhile I would say a few words or read some excerpts out of my book, *Silent Cry*. I agreed. Someone introduced me to the audience as a person who wanted to plug a book. After such a bad introduction, the audience gave me less than a warm welcome; the 400-plus people stared blankly at me. Their looks said to me, "Get off the stage, you're not Susan Taylor." As I started speaking, my confidence went down to nothing. As I began to read from my book, my body language said I couldn't wait to get off the stage. At my conclusion, a handful of the people gave applause. I stayed around and saw the difference in the way Susan was received by the same audience. She spoke about belief and confidence in oneself. That night, Susan autographed and sold hundreds of books; I sold one.

Practice Points:
- Be sure of who's introducing you
- Never lose your confidence in front of an audience

Apologies for wrong doings

Even though business had slowed down, I continued meeting different people from all social and economic backgrounds and experiences. Now I began to relax and enjoy the business. I started receiving letters from kids all over the city and state that said my words influenced their lives. These letters kept my personal disappointments in perspective for me.

Because I was constantly dealing with the public, I constantly ran across old associates from the housing projects or classmates from high school and college who knew me from my younger, wilder days.

Like me, you may have changed over the years and now want to have closure to some wrongs you have done to others by clearing the air with those people you had issues with. I personally took the opportunities to tell them that I had made mistakes. I sincerely apologized to them and asked if we could move on from what happened in the past to a better relationship now.

In my travels, I kept coming across women and men I had said something foolish to or disrespected years earlier with my then-foolish pride, immaturity and low self- esteem. These apologies had given me a new lease on life and also a sense of relief.

How much old baggage are you holding on to? What will it take for you to tell everyone you care about or hurt the way you feel? You have to start the process by going to them first; then you'll receive. It might be a spouse you had a fight with or a child you haven't expressed your love. When you put your arms around them, they'll soon put their arms around you. This selfless and humbling act frees you from the grip of fault and blame. It puts you in a position of strength because others see you are willing to admit to past mistakes. Now you can grow and move on to complete your life's purpose.

Preach Points:
- What keeps you humble?
- Clear the air
- Apologies put you in the position of strength

Letters of gratitude

As a speaker, trainer and writer, I've had the opportunity to share all my wisdom, values and passions with people who wanted to become better in their own lives. Over 200,000 people across the country have now heard my words. But the relationships my speaking has helped the most with are my relationships with my older sisters and brothers and other extended family.

Being the youngest of nine children, I always earned a certain reputation, especially at the family gatherings. My older siblings never let me grow up in their eyes, always treating me as just their little brother. Even after I married Donna, some of them actually felt sorry for her, because they thought she didn't know what she had gotten herself into. I knew they didn't understand me and they weren't interested in seeing my personal growth. I often considered that maybe my growing up meant their getting older.

Experts agree that one of the greatest needs a person has is the need to be listened to and understood. We all have a story to tell, and we all shine when others understand that story.

Now as a public speaker and writer, my family, like the public, became aware of my abilities. They all became involved in one way or another. My fourth-oldest sibling, Elouise, read my book, and wrote the most wonderful letter I've ever received. I call it a *letter of gratitude,* a letter thanking and appreciating me for being myself. This letter goes wherever I go because it lifts me up when I feel sad.

Dear E. J.:

After completing the reading of your book, I was compelled to write to you. I am feeling so much, I'm not sure how to start. First let me say that I am terribly proud of you. These words really don't express it all. I had mixed feelings about reading the book, even though I am an avid reader, because I have never been challenged with reading something so close to my own life. Actually it is my life, written by a part of me, that I now realize I knew very little about.

My heart was touched over and over again as I learned about your struggles and disappointments. It ached when I realized that I was never there for you. To learn that you had to carry so much by yourself left me feeling both painful and disappointed with myself. I want to apologize for not being more of a support to you. I guess I always saw you as a tower of strength needing no help from a big sister.

I was able to relate with so much that I read about. I can remember your visits home from college, and your excitement about football. I will never forget Ray and Deke; they have left impressions on my mind and heart that can never be erased. As I continued through, I would ask myself why God spared you so many times. I believe that God has a real purpose for all of us and yours has become very clear.

As I neared the end and the struggles did not seem to end, what impressed me was that you didn't stop. You continued on to reach your dream, and to serve your fellow brother, which is why we are all here.

I have lived long enough to know there is a power that supersedes man. It is my faith in God, not a church, religion, or person, that has assured me of my redemption through His son Jesus Christ.

I can't say enough how proud I am of you and what you are doing. You have decided to take a stand, alone if you have to, to make a difference. You have truly been given a wonderful gift. Thank you for being such a wonderful brother. I hope I can be here for you today and in the future.

I can't complete this letter without saying something about your wonderful wife. Few women understand how important is to support their husbands. Donna needs to know that without her support you could not have achieved this goal. Don't ever take her for granted. She is a gift, and one that is very hard to find.

THANKS FOR BEING MY BROTHER!

Your sister with love,
Elouise

The Ten Principles

Like Elouise, I learned to write letters of gratitude, as I wrote this letter to the older brothers of the Ray and Deke. I wrote it but never sent the letter to them. So I'm sending it in this book.

To My "Brothers" Brothers,

Dear Kevin and Keith Kennedy, the big brothers of Garry "Deke" Kennedy, and Eugene "Ivory" Grandberry, the big brother of Ray Anthony Grandberry,

Thanks be to the Creator of the worlds for big brothers like you. On today, 8-23-95, I had spent most of the day feeling sorry for myself, wondering if I had done the right thing by attempting to put the memories of your beloved brothers, Ray Anthony Grandberry and Garry Dean Kennedy into a book.

Because I loved them both unconditionally, and they both had given me so much, I couldn't accept not letting the world know who they were. I know my love for them couldn't match the three of you, because yours is the love of family.

But in my heart I wanted to do what I believed was right. I had the pleasure of speaking to all three of you extensively about my dreams and plans to make this book a reality. I spoke to both Kevin and Ivory just today. I wanted all three of you to know that the support you gave me will give me the energy and courage to speak out against violence and share a message of responsibility, respect and love.

I want all three of you to know that you are with me every time I say your little brothers' names. I love you as my own big brothers, and your confidence in me will make the difference for me to share with others.

Peace and love,

E.J. Bassette

Practice What You Preach

List five people to whom you would like to express gratitude

1._____
2._____
3._____
4._____
5._____

Now take one person from that list of five people and commit to writing a letter to them. Pull out a piece of paper, along with a stamp and envelope. Don't do like I did. Do like my sister, Elouise and mail that letter off today.

Practice Points:
- Be kind to others
- Apologize to others
- Go out of your way to make others feel comfortable
- Use unconditional love
- Often there is a problem with the system, not the people. Don't put good people into bad situations

8. Tell & Sell Your Story

"People seldom improve when they have no other
model but themselves to copy after."
-Goldsmith-

Practice What You Preach

<u>Telling & selling is part of the game</u>

Now with over five years of experience in the public speaking and professional training business, I constantly tried to adjust my plans by practicing the first seven principles of walking the walk and talking the talk by

1. Starting where you are today
2. Develop your philosophy and ideas
3. Operating out of your values and principles
4. Taking responsibility for your own life
5. Create a personal mission statement, a dream list and a goal sheet.
6. Seek out a balanced life
7. Create and build lasting relationships

The eighth principle entails learning and having the ability to tell and sell yourself and your story to others. Before you read on, I want you to know that you already are in the business of selling whether you consciously practice it or not. You're probably saying to yourself, "I'm not good with people and I certainly can't see myself trying to sell others by smiling and being pushy." But people who practice what they preach are master sellers. So, let me give you my definition of selling.

Selling is simply building and maintaining relationships with others, so that you can share mutual services with each other. In essence, you are already selling yourself in your day-to-day relationships, whether it's meeting a mate, sitting in a job interview, trying out for a sports team, or trying to get your children to eat the dinner you've prepared.

Becoming a master salesperson is only possible if you are making a conscious decision to communicate. I'm not talking about the old-fashioned concept of sales people who were fast-talking, untrustworthy characters trying to sell you a used car or vacuum cleaner. Those traits have given the concept of selling a black eye. A master seller has passionate stories, ideas, concepts, beliefs and principles. Do you get the picture?

There is no better feeling than to have others believe in what you say, stand for and are trying to accomplish.

Even on a professional selling level, some experts believe that over 30 million people are salespeople, and 50 million people use selling techniques in their professions. Even though, not everyone sells for a living, more of us need to consciously practice the same skills in order to get the results we want for ourselves and others.

But you may ask, "What is it I'm trying to sell?" You would be selling the best product in the world each and every day-yourself. When you're sharing your desires, needs and wants, the more you understand the power of selling, the more you'll see your life move in the direction you've planned. Remember, people help you because they like you and know you. Be excited to share your powerful story wherever you go.

Embrace the concept of selling as a technique that makes it easier for you to get the things you want and desire. Again, although this skill is all around, you still may not understand the power of how it works. For example, there's a principle that you may be familiar with called "*six degrees of separation*." The concept says that everyone you meet is six people away from somebody else you know. In other words, by talking, sharing, listening and learning, you'll find out the friends of friends. Imagine, if you could break the code of meeting the friends of friends. With the right dream and proper plan, you can't be stopped. This creates a common ground, setting the stage for trust and belief in you and where your dreams are headed. That can take you a long way when you're trying to get others to back your dreams.

To sell, you have to become an expert at communicating with others by listening first and talking second. You would share extreme confidence, because you believe in your product more than anyone else. That belief causes you to share the excitement with others. You want them to experience the same joy that you have experienced.

To become a master salesperson, you have to find out personal things about people. You don't pre-judge, but instead ask open-ended questions that don't get a yes or no answer, and also encourage conversation.

By being up-front, you're always showing honesty and integrity and discussing the expectations of your relationship. People become attracted to you because they know you are sincere and honest. Remember, that like attracts like, so people of the same mind gravitate toward each other.

I'll never forget my brother Eddie, who has a very progressive mindset. He was talking to a stranger about business and life. Their conversation related similar experiences and even crossed a few familiar friends. At the end of the conversation, the man said in a very excited and sincere manner that he wanted to stay in touch with Eddie any way possible. Eddie told the gentleman to keep doing what he was doing and by that fact they would run into each other again. First, I thought Eddie was just being rude, or was blowing the man off. But time proved Eddie right: he saw the man again, because like minds do seem to continually be in the same place, doing the same things. Think about the people of different places and influences you interact with all the time as part of your bigger network.

Professional selling

When you are a professional career salesperson, there are things you can do to sell and keep your customer, like always having an attitude that you will under-promise and over-deliver. That will let people around you enjoy the little extra you bring to their lives. Learn to give more than they expect. If your service delivers more than they anticipated, you become the true winner.

There's a story about a baker who always gives his customers an extra thirteenth donut when they order a dozen.

Confused, one customer asked the baker why he would be crazy enough to give away free donuts.

Without hesitation, the baker replied, "It's easier to give one donut away and keep a happy customer than to get a new customer after someone takes your old customer away." In other words, do the little extra in the beginning, and the favor will be returned to you in the end.

Master salespersons practice and role-play scenarios so that when they come across similar real life situations they handle them smoothly. They practice patience and have empathy for others by putting themselves in other's shoes.

Other things to do in order to win and influence people is to find out their birthdays, anniversaries or other special occasions and regularly send them cards. Network with people before they need your services. By sending thank-you notes, you show people that you are considerate of the time they shared with you. For instance, I'll never forget a client putting my thank-you card on her desk, displayed where everyone could see it. Do you think that may have made others like and trust me?

Preach Points:
- Make a conscious decision to communicate
- You already sell each day of your life
- Role-play scenarios before they happen

Don't oversell

Some people have a tendency of talking too much and taking over a conversation, or divulging too much information too quickly. That can make the other person uncomfortable, leaving the salesperson looking unprofessional, or even seeming out of control.

Others put their best face on long enough to get what they want, then stick a customer or friend with a bad product. That dishonest and deceitful move will only come back to have a negative effect. Always follow-up on promises long after the commitment. Master salespeople know that the work starts after the service, relationship or commitment is received: They go the extra mile.

> *Practice Points:*
> • Some people talk too much
> • Some people divulge too much information too quickly

First impressions

Shakespeare wrote that the world is a stage and we are simply playing a part on it.

This supports the fact that people are always watching, listening and making opinions, good or bad, about you. That's why the way you present yourself is a major key to your success. Have you ever wondered why others seem to get what they want out of life? Those people are aware that it is all in their presentation. Experts confirm that you make your greatest impact on others in the first 4 to 15 seconds after meeting, so remember: sometimes you don't get a second chance.

Steps to making a great first impression:
1. Have a friendly voice and smile.
2. Listen first, talk second.
3. Have a firm handshake & good eye contact.
4. Dress appropriately for your occasion.

Understanding behavior styles and personality traits

By learning your own personality traits and the traits of others, you will be able to deal with others on their terms because you will understand what it is they like and dislike. This will help you build stronger alliances with others, endearing yourself to them. Harvey Mackay, author of *How to*

Swim with the Sharks Without Being Eaten Alive uses the Mackay 66. These are fact-finding questions his salespeople utilize to learn about each of their business clients. His salespeople know everything, from their customers' favorite food to their birthdays. This techniques has given him great success in his multimillion-dollar envelope business.

In my team building workshops, I use behavior styles to get people to understand how to work with others whom they perceive as difficult. It's always fun to get the groups together to see who has what style. There are several styles that I find suitable. The first one is found in Tony Alessandra's book *The Platinum Rule.* Tony gives a unique look at the four basic personality types: Directors, Relaters, Socializers and Thinkers. Each one of these personality types carries a special set of traits that can be applied to understand yourself and others.

The second behavior style analysis I use is the D.I.S.C. system, developed by TTI, Ltd.[11] This system assesses a person for core behavior styles in Dominance, Influence, Steadiness, and Compliance. The results of this analysis are outstanding for job hiring, sales styles, team building, career pathing, supervisor, management and leadership development.

Houston Associates in Illinois and Phoenix is a distributor of the D.I.S.C. system. I'm presently a consultant for the Houston team. That allows me to have the latest information on human dynamics.

Positioning your product and services

Having your product or service available for customers puts you 80 percent in the game. By being in a position to actually deliver the product or service, you're 90 percent home. If you can deliver the product above and beyond expectations, you have positioned yourself and your product to have an *unfair*

---

[11] D.I.S.C. distributed by Target Training International, Ltd.

competitive advantage. The advantage gives your customer the right to say you have earned their business.

Remember, most people have ideas with no action or product, so that eliminates them from participating in the game. Secondly, most people lose sight of the customer, so delivery becomes slow. This not only drives customers crazy but also leaves them with a bad taste in their mouth. Further, most people over-promise and under-deliver, instead of the other way around. By under-delivering, you leave customers dissatisfied and not looking to use your product or services again.

Always position yourself to become an expert in your industry. You become an expert by knowing your product or service and what drives your customer to do business with you. You must also find out what in your industry is difficult for your competition but comes easy for you. This information will give you that unfair competitive advantage, putting you in the best position to serve and keep the customer.

Always position yourself as a person who gives praise and recognition to others, pushing them to come out winners. Achieving this leaves people with experiences of feeling good about their decision to use your product or service.

Customers have to always be able to answer these questions about you and your services before they can justify doing business with you. Why should I do business with you? Why would you benefit doing business with me? Here are other questions that have to be answered:

• *What is different about your product?* What do you have that someone can only get from you? You have to ask the question, Why would they want to buy from me? or What will make them use what I have over the next person's product? This is also true with respect to you. What makes you different or unique from the next person? Why should somebody marry you or hire you or do anything with you? Find out what it is

180

about your product and services that puts you head and shoulders above everyone else.

• *What is your major strength?* By knowing your strengths, you allow others to emulate and become part of what works well for you. Your strengths will be rooted in your principles and values. I learned a long time ago that it's better to put your best foot forward and let others see your high points.

• *Who are the customers for your product?* By knowing about your product, you need to find the people who would most benefit from what you have to offer. Remember, a person will enjoy you and your product more if they have a need.

• *80/20 Rule* This rule says that the top 20 percent of your customers will generate 80 percent of the sales. So concentrate on taking care of your top customers. That doesn't mean you forget about the rest. Know where your business is coming from and who your very best customers are. Remember, it's easier to keep an old customer than to go out and get a new one.

• *1\3 rule (call to sale ratio).* You're not going to ever get all of the business that is out there, but let's look at a ratio of how to estimate your anticipated business. Picture all the business being thrown into a hat. For the sake of this point, say there are 9 accounts you are trying to get into your product. The one-third rule says 3 accounts will use your services, 3 will say "I'll use you at a later date and 3 will never do business with you. This call-to-sale ratio gives you an excellent way to gauge how many decision makers you need to meet in order to have enough sales.

• Make guarantees; back them up. Make guarantees and promises that lend to the credibility of your services. Just back up your guarantees with action. When you are positioning yourself, understand there will be a sales cycle that you'll have to learn. At first, sales may move slowly because there is not enough history of you or your product to give you name recognition. During these times, stick with your warm leads and familiar markets. Continue to practice the law of consistency and stay with it.

Remember the standard rule of business is that the first three to five years will be like a roller coaster. So, position yourself for the long term and have a good plan. Remember, it may take a good ten years before you can say your business is successful.

<u>There are four stages of business competence</u>

• *Unconscious Incompetence:* You don't know what you're doing is wrong, and you don't know enough to know why it's wrong.

• *Conscious Incompetence*: You are aware you're doing something wrong, but don't know why.

• *Unconscious Competence:* You are doing something right, but don't know why it's right.

• *Conscious Competence:* You know you are doing it right, and you know why and how you are doing it right.

<u>What is your story? People help you when they know you</u>

In each personal and professional development workshop I've conducted, at some point the participants are asked to meet other people they don't know in the room. Normally, their uncomfortable reactions turn into continuous conversation about things they have in common. I've even had a few people find out they were related to each other. By sharing your personal story, others relate to your journey and start sharing your story with even more people. Earlier in my sales career, during a casual conversation, I shared my story with a married couple. My desire was to get into a different industry. The couple felt a need to help and thus introduced me to a person in a position to get me a job. By my sharing my story, they were able to help change the course of my life.

Unfortunately, most stories are told too late. Many people don't take the time to write, share or believe who they are and what matters most to them. So their story goes to the cemetery, along with their dreams and ambitions.

Most experts will agree that one of the greatest needs human beings have is the desire to be listened to and understood. But again, because people have so little hope in their dreams, they leave the planet never sharing their story with the majority of people they meet. Instead, their dreams are written in obituaries, to be told after they are gone. Their story is simply left to the interpretation of others.

If you are practicing what you preach, your story is being told by you while you are here to tell it. Others will pick up on your story, as well as various people of importance who will begin believing and being part of it. That's when you're called an overnight success. People like Oprah, Michael Jordan, Nelson Mandela, President John Kennedy and Dr. Martin Luther King, all have stories that are being told. Remember, all of us have a story to tell. What is yours?

Having a powerful story is not just for the rich and famous, so don't be intimidated by your own truth and try to hide your story from the rest of the world. Many people find it very difficult to share the facts about their circumstances with others for fear they are revealing too much, when in fact that is the exact opposite. First of all, you don't belong to just yourself, you belong to a higher power. Second, your sharing may help someone else who has been walking the same path as you. Third by sharing, you help heal your wounds and move on to bigger and better things.

Because your story is uniquely yours, it doesn't mean you're the only one to have similar experiences. I always marvel at the victims from the Holocaust, as they tell the horrendous acts that were perpetrated on them during World War II. As painful as the stories were, they are told repeatedly by the victims so that others will never forget. Through the pain, many of the victims are able to help others deal with their own losses. Your pain can help someone else grow. I'm shocked that so many parents don't talk with their children about the mistakes they made in their lives. They hide the very things that would bring about respect and understanding from their kids.

In the sharing of my life in the book *Silent Cry,* as well as public speaking, I've received letters from people sharing their thoughts about my work. A letter from a lady in her forties who read my book expressed her feelings of growing up in Chicago's housing projects. She now considers herself a success and had tried to escape her past because she was embarrassed and ashamed of the stigma the inner-city projects carried. She felt that people would judge her differently if they knew from where she came. But, by reading my story, she realized that those experiences were the part of her life that gave her character and taught her how to handle struggle and pain. She learned to be tough when life demanded it from her. My story made her feel proud of her total life and especially her deep secret about living in the projects. She said that she would forever be a different person.

Preach Points:

Unfortunately, most stories are told too late
Don't leave your story for the interpretation of others
Through your pain others will grow

The power of words

In order for her to reach that point, she had to practice self-love, self-acceptance and self appreciation. That starts when you are able to say and think nice things about yourself to yourself. It is said that 80 percent of our thoughts about ourselves are negative. We spend more time talking ourselves out of things than believing we can accomplish them. By the time we are adults, we have heard the word "no" thousands of times. Words have so much power in them, and we often use them to limit ourselves. So, we have to reprogram ourselves to think positive.

List five power words about yourself that describe your greatness.

1._____
2._____
3._____
4._____
5._____

List 3 words you will never use again to negatively describe yourself.

1._____
2._____
3._____

I knew a doctor who felt pain and anger because he wouldn't share his story and his brother's life with his colleagues. Because his brother was on drugs, he hid from the fear of what his medical community might think of him, leaving him embarrassed and confused. I helped him understand that he was carrying too much of a burden. By sharing his story, he was able to seek professional advice and acceptance.

As I had continued to tell my story around the country, the theory of six degrees of separation came into full effect. I began to meet and participate in events and workshops with some of the people I had once read about in papers, books and magazines. For example, I was invited to sit on a panel discussing family values. One of the people on the panel was

Rev. Jesse Jackson, the first black man to seriously run for President of the United States. A few others that have been able to hear me speak or get a copy of *Silent Cry*: singer Jerry "Ice Man" Butler; former Chicago Bears football players, Chris Zorich and Dave Duerson; author and founder of Athletes against Drugs, Stedman Graham; Representative Maxine Waters; and television news personalities, Harry Porterfield, Cheryl Burton and Bill Campbell. And a host of others.

Take a moment and write out some of the positive things you have accomplished in your life. Write your own story your way.

My Story :

_____

_____
_____
_____
_____
_____
_____
_____

No test no testimony

In telling your story, have a compelling way to convey it to your listener. A winning story has to go through all the phases of overcoming the overwhelming. People are more apt to listen to someone who's been in the trenches and knows first-hand what it's like. So, don't skip a phase of your journey because your captive audience would not be fully aware of the significance or greatness. In other words, no one knows you as well as yourself.

By *self-analysis*, you will learn that you have held on to some difficulties in the past and never resolved them. You will realize that when you didn't see a way out, through self-analysis you found that small ray of hope and pushed yourself through. In other words, in order to get to heaven you might have felt like you just went through hell. What makes your story worth telling is the fact that you understood what it took to get where you are now.

In sports we tend to cheer for the underdog, the athlete who struggled. No one believed in him or her but themselves. They relate to us because they fought and scratched their way from the bottom. The process of life prepares you for all the great things you're going to receive. Prominence before you have paid your dues and proved yourself will not leave you with the hunger to sustain your success. You may not always get what you want but you can make the best out of what you have.

Practice Points:

- Tell your story in a compelling way
- You can find hope and push yourself through
- You may not get exactly what you want

Have mentors and coaches

You must have people who buy into you, people who are willing to take a chance on your product, services or skills. They are people who are doing well in the area where you're trying to make a difference. This is called the *theory of relative existence* or *centers of influence*. This means you need friends in high places, friends who believe in you, who can help take your mission to the next level. Either they are the end user of what you are offering, or they are capable of teaching you the ins and outs of the market you're in. They can also share your efforts with others, because they are well known and respected. They carry a lot of power and influence with others.

You can call them mentors or role models or coaches because they take you under their leadership. Without them, you can find yourself taking years trying to do something that they could teach and expose you to in a fraction of the time.

Usually a mentor is someone who loves to see others get ahead, someone well known and successful in the area you're trying to master. The mentor's joy is often in seeing you grow, and knowing that he or she had a hand in your development and success. I know that wherever I travel around the state of Illinois, someone will share with me the joy they received from either hearing me speak before or having read my first book. I know that this couldn't have happened without me believing in my story enough to share it with others. But even with me believing, I had to have friends, family, businesspeople and mentors who believed in me.

I have so many people who have believed in me over the years. People like Dr. Kim Muhammad–Earl of the Chicago Public School system who uses my services and supports my work. Ms. Bobbie Green and Doris J. Odem also come to mind. Dr. Winston Johnson, Phil Jackson, President and CEO of Boys & Girls Clubs of Chicago and founder of Black Star Youth Foundation, as well as hundreds of principals and teachers, event coordinators, business owners, ministers like the late Pastor Lawrence Mosley, who have given me an opportunity to speak in front of their students, staffs, congregations and business professionals. You have to find mentors and role models who believe in what you're doing, or those who are doing what you want to do.

Other speakers, like Mark Sanders of Chicago, have been helpful in sharing tips and information about the business, as well as sharing leads on getting new business. Jerry and Julie Houston of Houston Associates, an organization that maximizes potential in employees' personal and professional lives, have had a great impact on my overall professional development.

Your mentors and coaches then become part of your larger network. And again they all play a part in the big picture you are trying to paint. Other people in my network I would like to consider includes family and friends. Dad and my sisters and brothers, Elleana, Eddie, Earina, Elouise, Eldora, Elaine and

Eric. Brother and sister in laws Annette, Joyce, Fred, James, Willie, Robert, Sam, and of course my wife Donna. Pat and Arthur Chaney are excellent role models from New Jersey. Corporate employees from companies such as Lucent Technologies, AT&T, Preferred Staffing and many others have been invaluable to my development.

Name some mentors in your life

1._____

2._____

3._____

What do you need from them to get to the next level?

The courage of life

Unlikely people will come into your life at unlikely times and show you what giving support to others unselfishly is all about. This experience came to mind when I met the late Joe Gardner of the Chicago Water Reclamation Committee, who was running on the Democratic ticket for mayor of Chicago against the powerful incumbent, Mayor Richard Daley. With little support, and even less money, Joe continued his mission to become mayor. During Joe's campaign, he stopped in at an event I was attending and I gave him a copy of *Silent Cry*.

As time passed, his bid for mayor proved unsuccessful. I was impressed by the letter he wrote thanking me for sharing my book with him. After reading the book, he was convinced I needed to be recognized for my work. He took the initiative to invite me to the Reclamation Committee meeting to receive an award for trying make a difference. It was an experience that I'll never forget. A few years later, I read that Joe had died. I was never aware of the illness that he had. I was impressed with a man who spent his time doing what he believed and being a true mentor. Despite his challenges, he still gave to others.

Practice What You Preach

Preach Points :
- People will give you support at unlikely times
- Even with challenges, still give to others

Don't judge a book by its cover

We all are guilty of prejudging others by the way they look, how they dress or the color of their skin. When you learn to practice what you preach, you'll know the principles that won't allow you to judge others inappropriately. If you're truly living on the highest level of consciousness, you know to treat everyone with respect. Successful people have the ability to walk with kings, while simultaneously relating to the common person. You may wonder why the person with tremendous success seems to gain the trust of others. It is because he truly practices the law of *treat your brother the way he would like to be treated.*

Have you ever had someone treat you badly just because they didn't know you? I'm always amazed at the number of people who operate out of suspicion. Being a speaker, I've often experienced the prejudging agenda of others, first-hand. Before speaking engagements, I routinely walk throughout the audience, talking to people but not announcing that I'm the speaker. I could be the nicest person in the world and I'll run into that person or people who treat me with suspicion, as if I just stole their first-born. I love seeing the look on their faces when I'm introduced to the podium. That look of "I didn't know you were that guy." I've learned to look past it and even have used it as a *teaching moment.* Think about someone you've prejudged.

I've learned my lesson about inappropriately prejudging. I felt sorry for a middle-age lady working in a shop that I frequented. I always thought that she worked too hard and presumed she was too old to work for such little money. While at a donut shop, I saw the poor lady working a second job. I

190

would talk to her out of pity, while disguising my concern. During a brief conversation with her one day, she requested my advice. She said, "I'm really getting tired of trying to be in two places. What do you think I should do, sell this place or the donut shop?" My mouth dropped and I began to smile uncontrollably. She *owned* the two businesses. I learned my lesson not to prejudge.

Preach Points:
- Successful people can walk with kings and the common person
- Don't prejudge people

Become a master student

In order to operate at the highest level, you have to become a master student of life, information and ideas. One of the great tools a student possesses is the ability to learn from others, sparing the time it takes to reinvent the wheel. Learning from great people's experiences will speed up your learning curve by years. Someone once said, "It is great to learn from your own mistakes, but it is ingenious to learn from the mistakes of others."

The greatest lesson a parent instills in a child is the sharing of experiences. We've all heard our parents say things like, "When I was your age," or "I've been there and done that." By experience and repetition, parents are able to drive messages into their children over the years, drilling the conscious and subconscious values they believe most important. I know my mom and dad drove into me the concept of hard work and never making excuses. Dad, a World War II veteran, didn't want to hear a lot of belly-aching and complaining. By being a master student, you're able to absorb those messages and learn that they are blessings to guide you through life.

Throughout my seminars, I raise the question of how have we learned from those lessons taught. I'm astonished that many

191

of my participants hear the message, but few practice and respond with action to become masters over their own affairs.

The best way to learn from others' experiences is through the power of books. Others have taken the time to leave us a lifetime of information and resources. You have to understand the power of positive words. The words you let into your subconscious can empower or dis-empower you. The information in those books is worth thousands or even millions of dollars, and you can purchase it in a book for $20 or $30.

As I mentioned earlier, Oprah Winfrey, one of the most successful and wealthiest women in the world, often reflects on how, as a little girl, books took her on journeys around the world. Although she grew up in poverty, it was experiences of others through books that made her a student of life and the world. Books allowed her to see past the limitations put on her. Remember: almost everything you want to know is in the library, and the information there is free to use. All you have to do is find it.

To become a master student, it takes discipline and requires you to give up unproductive habits, while moving toward things that will unleash new horizons and destinies. Master students avoid dangers while mastering opportunities. Learn not to allow the highs to take you too high and the lows to get you too low. This will keep you even- tempered, not causing massive mood swings, or in effect, creating a burn-out mentality.

Practice Points:
- Master life by mastering information and ideas
- Learn from the power of books
- Becoming a master student takes discipline

Do you have to live large to be happy?

You have to develop a definition of what success means to you. Without one, other people will define it for you. Even though they're not in your field and have never done what you

192

are doing. Many people will try to advise you on what to do. So keep the right information and resources in front of you, while making the proper discussions. For instance, people are always advising me to be on the Oprah Winfrey show. But they can't give me a contact person or a feasible plan. So I have to stick to the best plan I have, not changing it every time someone wants to change it for me. Remember, stick with the plan that works.

Practice Points:
- • Have your definition of success
- • Stick with the plan that works

Teamwork

People who practice what they preach usually operate well within the team concept. Although teams are made up of individuals, they function as one while accomplishing a common goal. The effort they put forth while together is called teamwork. This same cooperation is experienced in your family life, work environment and social and community life.

A good example of teamwork is seen in the field of track during a 4x100 relay race. To win a meet, this 4x100 team spends hours learning how to work together. A person can only run his or her part of the race, then he or she passes the baton to the next runner. It takes all four runners to complete the relay or race at the fastest time to reach the highest level of winning. The same teamwork is required in the race of life where our job is to find others who share the same values, desires, commitments and dreams. Most importantly, by practicing the ultimate team-work, you can keep the baton of life moving forward to the next generation.

Practice Points:
- • Teams are made up of individuals
- • Keep the baton moving to the next generation

How to build a successful team

The team you build is critical in helping you practice all that you preach. The team has to have all the resources available in order to help make the team competitive. And the team has to be able to compete for the desired outcome you're looking for. The teammates can range from family, friends, mentors and role models-all of the people you need to get to the highest level. I like to call these people your *"all-star team."* When you think of all-stars, you think of the best at what they do. By surrounding yourself with the best, you learn their secrets to success.

The best have the most valuable assets which are called *resources*. The resources may include marketing tools, financial information or expertise in a particular area. Those resources are critical in reaching the desired outcome you're looking for. Remember, if you are headed in one direction and your team is headed in another, somebody is wasting a lot of time, money and effort. With all the elements of a team working together, you have the proper blend for success.

The L. A. Lakers were the first team to win a basketball championship in the new millennium. Each player used his individual abilities and resources to have the same outcome and goal of winning a championship. Here is a breakdown of how their teamwork worked.

Made up of individuals
- Got the right players to play the parts
- Picked the right coaching staff

Used their resources
- Have a game plan
- Had an offense that was geared toward their strength
- Did all the little things right

A common desired outcome
- Made clear the expectations to win
- They all wanted to win a championship

194

This example also makes scoring off the court critical, because the best baskets are made in the game of life. Those points start with your family members. Remember, the best way to win is to be proactive, not reactive.

Do you know each of the roles you and your teammates play? How have you positioned yourself on your team?

List 3 things going well on your team.

1._____
2._____
3._____

List 3 things that need improvement

1._____
2._____
3._____

What strengths do you add?

1._____
2._____

What strengths do you lack?

1._____
2._____

What strengths do other teammates add?

1._____
2._____

Practice Points:

- Teams are made up of individuals
- The teammates can range from family, friends, mentors and role models
- Team-work has to have the proper blend for success.

Take your mission where others refuse to go:

Now that you know how to successfully sell yourself, have found mentors and developed a team, you can take your skills on the road. If you believe your product or service is good, you should be willing to use it with the toughest clients, not just the easy ones. You should be excited to give it to anyone who wants to hear it, see it or utilize it. That is what I did with my motivational training.

I found out about the Midnight Basketball Leagues of Chicago through the founder, Gil Walker, of the Chicago Housing Development. He called on me to assist in motivating and inspiring young men to stay off the streets. Midnight Basketball was formed many years ago so the young men in the inner city would have safe places to go and things to do after dark. Because of the vision of one man, Gil Walker, Midnight Basketball became a reality all over Chicago.

Gil became aware of my work and asked me to speak before their games. The games required me to go into the Chicago Housing Projects at 10:30 p.m. This is a job that most people would turn down. But contrary to what most people would think, the young men were very nice and well mannered. They received me well and asked me to come back. I've taken them up on their offer and made repeated visits.

Practice Points:
- Take your skills on the road
- If you believe in your product or service, use it in the toughest situations

9. Become a Problem Solver

"Opportunity… often it comes in the form of misfortune or temporary defeat."
-Napoleon Hill-

If you have read and completed all of the exercises from chapter one to this point, you have made and become aware of some significant changes in your life. If you haven't taken the time to attempt the exercises, you have missed a perfect opportunity to expand your growth. Remember, nothing works unless you work it. You have the opportunity to enrich your life by fulfilling the intentions the Creator put you on the earth to do. Your purpose is clear, and you are following the life you designed for yourself. In other words, you are beginning to live a joyous life with the *highest standards*. By living and setting the highest standards, you are no longer willing to accept less than this life has to offer. You see that the more productive your life is, the more value has been added, bringing a total fulfillment in each and every day.

You might also notice an increased pressure to produce positive outcomes. This pressure has to be managed in order for you to handle the greater demand you and others will have for your newly unleashed talents and expectations.

> "That to which much is given, much is required."
> -Bible-

Become the leader you're looking for

Since you have become more in harmony with your values, goals and purpose, carrying them out day-to-day will bring attention to you. Practicing what you preach, day in and day out, will put you in the top 10 percent of winners in this country. Others will see the change. Co-workers and family members will notice the difference in your attitude and the way you handle yourself. People will, in fact, start gravitating to you and asking your advice because of your commitments to what you believe.

In short, people are looking for leaders to help them solve all the problems and situations that they face. People simply need answers to some of the complicated problems they face. You may say "I'm not the one," but the fact that you are standing up for what you believe gives you an obligation to be counted on. And guess what? Just continue to practice what you preach and you'll see yourself rising to the challenge, in spite of your own doubts. In the Bible, many of God's prophets, like Moses and Noah, didn't think they could deliver what God wanted. But because of their discipline and faith, they were more prepared for the challenge than even they knew and expected.

By practicing what you preach, you have already put yourself in a position to become part of the *solution* instead of part of the *problem*. That leaves the others feeling helpless and looking for what you have. You must turn to sharing with them your gifts of what should be done.

So, in essence, you become a leader who then sets himself or herself apart by being a problem solver. A leader or coach is not just the person that people see in front. They are persons who serve others. Most people confuse the word leadership with authority. Blind authority can be superficial and arrogant, leading you, your family or business down a path of disaster. But real leaders know the first quality of true leadership is that of service. Think about all the great leaders who came to serve humankind, who had a vision for improving humanity. There are also millions of leaders around the world leading their families to success.

Following are other traits to help you become a true leader

1. Be appreciative and humble: Leaders sacrifice their own for the good of the whole. Put others first.

2. Begin with praise and honest appreciation: Leaders always begin their conversations with positive input.

Practice What You Preach

3. Call attention to other's mistakes indirectly: Don't make a scene. Allow others to learn without being humiliated.

4. Talk about your own mistakes before criticizing the mistakes of others: Share that you are not above mistakes.

5. Speak to the issue, not to the person: resolve the problem without alienating the individual.

Practice Points:
- Become more in harmony with your values
- Leaders are persons that serve others
- Blind authority can be superficial and arrogant

"Don't waste today out of fear for tomorrow."
-E.J. "Edge" Bassette-

Problem solver

You are put into a leadership position because of one thing and one thing only. That reason is your ability to solve problems, while getting the results needed. This makes being proactive and keeping your word vital to problem solving. Some people make a living on confusion, fear, destruction and blinded leadership. Their true goal is to keep their audience in the dark. But the Bible teaches us that where there is no light there is darkness. Where there is light, there is truth, and truth is knowledge.

Then there are those who take information and make bad choices. Instead of having the ability to take a problem, analyze it, and solve it, they simply can't make good decisions. Now I'm a big believer that the Creator gave us all the ability to make choices and He shows us at given times how to decide the truth. It still takes us to make the proper decision based on those choices. We have to practice common sense, which comes with experience that leads to good judgment.

Here is a story I like to tell that gives you an example of what I mean. A man caught in a flood, instead of driving away, decided to stay. His neighbors asked him to jump into their car, but he turned them down, saying God would take care of him. As his house began flooding, he ran outside and sat on the top of his car to escape the water. A boat full of people floated by and offered him a ride. The man turned them down, as he shouted to them that God would take care of him.

In the meantime, the water continued to rise, so high that the man had to get on the roof of his house. Just in the nick of time, a helicopter spotted him and tried to throw a ladder down so he could be rescued. He refused to get on, saying God was in control and would take care of him to see him through. Eventually, the water overtook him. He drowned and went to heaven, where he stood before God.

The man was confused and angry. He asked God why he left him in his time of need. God replied, "I sent you a car, a boat and a helicopter, and you refused them all." The moral of the story is that some people don't have a clue. They lack common sense to make those critical decisions.

In my youth seminars with young people in the inner city, I teach them that they have the best opportunity to solve the problems in their community. They are always stunned to hear me say they are in the best position in the world. I go on to teach them that with all the problems in the community, the community has to be saved from the inside out, not the outside in. I convince them that once others see them trying to solve their own problems, they'll join efforts to help them. In other words, if you don't care, they won't care.

I teach them to view every corner that has an abandoned building as a chance for them to become a real-estate owner. When they see a lack of adequate healthcare, they should consider becoming a doctor, a nurse or some other healthcare professional. Through empowerment, they learn how to problem solve. I'm not in the business of teaching dependency. Problem solving is concentrating 10% on the problem and 90% on the solutions.

The same is true for businesses, professional associations, companies and your personal life. You must have "how-to action steps" that you can take right away and see results. Always make solutions not excuses for your problems.

<u>*Practice Points:*</u>
- The Creator gave us all the ability to make choices
- Some people make a living on confusion, fear, destruction and blinded leadership
- Problem solving is concentrating 10% on the problem and 90% on the solutions

<u>Respect for self</u>

In order to be a problem solver, you have to have respect for yourself first, then others will respect you. You begin by looking at situations and seeing the glass half-full, instead of half-empty. That means you will always see more than one way to view a circumstance. The first way is to see a circumstance with the glass half-empty, or with all its faults. Viewing a situation with this outlook gives you the bleakest, darkest, picture you can paint. This perspective leaves little room for improving the matter, and you'll eventually give up. This outlook will also have you looking at situations-regardless of whether it's your life, job, family or finances-from a point of weakness, not strength.

On the other hand, if you approach the same situation and see the glass as half-full, you'll always give yourself a chance to make even the bleakest circumstances work out. This will propel you to keep looking for solutions in a positive, upbeat manner.

Both of these outlooks play a significant part in the way you attack a problem and how you view yourself. When you care for yourself in a self-respecting manner, you tend to have a more positive demeanor. You will act out your thoughts through your body language. You will look in the mirror and have a better self-reflection than a person who is not self-respecting. *Self-respect* is the key to loving who you are, what you stand for, as well as your overall self-esteem. Other people will react to you based on the respect you have for yourself. Even your children can detect whether or not you have what it takes.

I think back to when my son, Mario was about eight-years-old. After playing with a friend, Mario had to come home because the sun was starting to go down. While sitting on the porch enjoying the summer night, he started reflecting on some concerns he had noticed at his friend's house. "Dad, why is John allowed to stay out after dark?" Before I could answer, he continued, "I don't think his parents care too much about his safety, because I see John leaving the neighborhood on his bike, and even riding it in the street. John's parents even allow him to scream at them and they don't even say anything back to him."

As I sat silently, he continued. "Dad, why does John's dad just sit in front of the television all the time smoking cigarettes and letting John talk like that to him? I don't think his dad is too happy because he does this all day. I don't think John respects his parents. Dad, I don't think John's dad respects himself." Without my having to ever say a word, my eight-year-old knew something was wrong, and it started with his friend's dad, not the son.

To keep practicing what you preach, you have to constantly test your respect level. Without self-love and a positive outlook, you can find yourself not having very good self-esteem.

Practice Points:
- Look at situations and see the glass as half-full
- Self-respect gives you higher self-esteem
- Your body language suggest to others who you are

Causes of problems

In companies, most problems stem from relationship difficulties starting at the top. The relationship conflicts need to be worked out. Even in family problems, a husband and a wife have to take the bulk of responsibility for the children. There are several factors that exist when a problem is prevalent.

The problem exists because of:
- A lack of positive communication
- Inability to act upon a problem
- The lack of positive attitudes
- Ignorance about the root cause of the problem
- Inability to separate the problem from the individuals
- A lack of creativity about alternatives

Because you solve one problem, don't think that another one won't come right behind it to take its place. In fact, problems will always exist, but how you handle them is what is going to make the ultimate difference. Once you understand that you should positively approach all your problems, you are halfway there.

"Don't worry about everything and take care of nothing"
-E.J. "Edge" Bassette-

No Quick Fixes

When solving problems, don't look for the easy answer or a quick fix. Try to ask the questions that will uncover the root cause of why something is going on. By looking for the root cause of the problem, you are indeed finding what's below the surface. For example, you may continually cut your fingers when you use kitchen knives to prepare dinner. You can't solve the problem by putting a bandage on the cut. The root cause of the problem is the way you handle the knife. The long-term solution might be to take a class or have someone teach you how to properly cut. This skill of problem solving will prove to be valuable in your quest to become unstoppable.

No matter where you are, your worth increases when you can develop these and other critical thinking skills. Remember again, the world is always looking for answers. I have done many seminars that teach people how to take control of their destiny, while polishing their life skills. I find many of them receptive to learning how to take a leadership role in their own lives. I find that critical thinking skills are also vital to individuals who get discouraged with what they see to be complex problems. So instead of complaining about the problems, we began to act on them. To take an action means to get involved with why the problem exists. To act on the problem also means you have to make a decision and choose a new direction.

Most people want the results or benefits of a problem being solved, but don't want to take part in having to make a decision. Decisions are difficult because there is a chance the proposed solution might not work, causing one to feel pain, rejection or fear. But don't bury your head in the sand. Acknowledge the problem. Confront the deeper issue. Get it on the table. A healthy way to accept challenges is not to ask for fewer problems but to ask for more wisdom to solve them. Find a method in your life to get what you want.

In many cases, I have had seminars in wealthy suburban communities where middle-school children have problems with sex, drugs, drinking and smoking. The parents and teachers don't admit that these problems occur in their community. So instead of acknowledging their kids' issues, they decided to bury their heads in the sand.

On one occasion, after I spoke in an affluent area, the kids from my training walked up to me and said the teachers didn't see the need for my presentation on drugs. The students shared with me that the teachers said bad things didn't happen in their town. But the kids shared with me their need for my message, regardless of what the faculty said, because they were being confronted daily with the issues of sex, drugs and alcohol. Parents and teachers need to stop sugar-coating life for our youth. They need to continually ask questions, address the issues and come up with alternatives for our children.

Practice points:
- Don't always look for an easy answer
- Learn critical thinking skills
- Acknowledge the problem

Put others first

Helping people empower themselves continued to drive my desire to help even more people. My speaking opportunities let me know there was something special about what I was doing. People continued to grow under my trainings, workshops and books. They expressed wishes of good health and peace, and to continue to let God guide me on this journey. As the places and faces started to add up, one theme kept coming to my attention. That was the level of pain that was in this country due to violence on the nation's children. Regardless of whether I spoke for the government, major corporations, schools or churches, some mother or sister or husband or wife would come up and say someone close in their family had been murdered, harmed or abused. These scenarios began to test my faith, as I often walked away feeling hopeless and helpless seeing frustration, pain and tears. My own prayers assured me

I was doing what God wanted me to do, as I continued to grow into a resource to be an instrument of change.

Preach Points:
- Help others to empower themselves
- We must stop the violence on our youth
- Continue to be an instrument of change

A misguided generation: "Class of 89"

Helping me work toward that instrument of change, my beliefs continued to be pushed by the despair that others seemed to go through. I carried the idea of being part of the solution to give me peace in what otherwise seemed like a dismal situation. I know I had my own journey through life that I discussed in detail in *Silent Cry,* which prepared me for some of the things I would hear or witness. But other things I heard or came across, I don't think I could ever get used to. One example of something that left me numb, was a conversation I had with an eighth-grade teacher of an inner-city school. She had an interest in my self-esteem training geared for the African-American males in her class.

She was particularly concerned because of the issues her young men were facing on a day-to-day basis because of the deteriorating factors in the community. She didn't want the same thing to happen to these boys that had happened to her graduation class of 1989. She explained that in that eighth-grade class, she had 13 boys. Then her voice dropped as she explained that after graduating, all 13 had been murdered before their twentieth birthdays. So within six years after elementary school, a generation of young men was dead.

I know in my heart they could have been saved with the right values; with positive exposure their experiences could have taken them to a positive path.

This great nation cannot continue to lose its most precious resource-its children.

Preach Points:
- Some things happen that you are not prepared for
- We can't keep losing our precious resources
- Everyone can be saved

Secret of achievement

Unfortunately, without being able to produce results consistently, others will tend to disregard you and your agenda. The perceived value of your services determines whether the results are justified. The value also becomes a life-long measure of whether you have put a winning sequence of events together. For instance, in sports, a team may have one winning season, but that in itself doesn't qualify them as a winning franchise. That winning season lets others know they are headed in the right direction. That same team would have to win year in and year out to be regarded as a winning franchise.

Anything else would be referred to as a "one-hit wonder" or a "flash in the pan." I guess one of the other forms of achievement is having a system that merits consistency.

Consistency in achievement is the only option. If it's worth the results, you'll do whatever it takes to complete the task.

People who put their heart into their passions develop a consistency and don't mind working late into the night or waking up early in the morning. It's similar to the excitement you had as a child waking up early Christmas morning anticipating the toys under the tree. You could not wait until morning because your mind was full of anticipation about what results or presents you would receive.

In order to get the best results, you must also know how to measure the quantitative results. Know what your breakeven point is and how you can maintain a level of success.

You've heard the saying, "It's easy to get to the top, but much more difficult to stay there." That's because many people lose the edge that made them determined and consistent.

Preach Points:
- Consistency is the secret
- Remember Christmas morning as a kid
- It's easy to get to the top, but hard to stay there

Don't ask others to clean your mess

We all go through a maturation process that allows us to gauge where someone in society should be, based on their age and other factors. This process starts when we are conceived in the mother's womb to the last moment on the planet, maturing consciously or unconsciously, even as you are reading this very moment. There are always internal pressures and external pressures, measuring what your level of maturity is, based on reality.

For example, you are always anticipating the way others should act, based on their age, experience and other factors. For instance, you will tolerate a whining child before you tolerate a whining adult. Adults have more external pressure on them to behave more maturely.

You may ask, "Why is it necessary to be conscious of maturing when it's going to happen anyway?" Again, by being aware you have the advantage and opportunity to actively be involved and participate and even excel in your own growth. Yes, by accelerating your own process, you can give yourself the things you desire at an earlier stage.

Most of us need that encouragement to go to the next stage of growth. It's just like the bird who pushes her young out of the nest to fly. She knows without giving her young that extra push, they will sit in the nest indefinitely, waiting to be fed. That, in itself, will produce destructive results, because the bird will not learn how to search for food on its own, leaving starvation as its only option. The same happens to us in the course of our lives. Many become self- motivated and directed, ready to leave the nest. Then there are those who just can't seem to leave the nest and continually need to be fed by others.

I have a story I'd like to share with you about how my son didn't want to progress to his next level of maturation. When he was small, Donna began training him to use the potty chair. Those of you who have children can relate to this story. After he finished, we told him to sit there and shout to us to come in and clean his bottom and put a fresh Pamper on him. So he would holler from the bathroom, "Mommy I'm finished, come and wipe my booty." Donna would stop what she was doing and go attend to his needs.

As time passed, he outgrew the potty-chair, but he didn't outgrow his call for Donna to clean him. I can still hear him now, "Mommy I need you to wipe my booty." And like good Old Faithful, Donna would stop what she was doing. As time continued, he had slowly turned from a baby to a little boy who should have been cleaning himself. But, because he had someone else do it for him, it was no problem for him to call on Donna. Finally, one day he hollered for her to come to the bathroom, and she said no. Donna hollered back for to him sit there until he cleaned himself. He just sat there and cried, because we had conditioned him to rely on us. I'm glad to say he did eventually do it for himself. Like my son, there are some of you still hollering for someone else to do for you what you can and must do for yourself.

Preach Points:
- We all anticipate the way others should act
- We all need to be kicked out of the nest
- Are you asking others to clean your mess?

210

10. Be Ready to Move On: Jump and the Net Will Appear

"The successful person will profit from his mistakes and try again in a different way"
-Dale Carnegie-

Time Management 101

You have *constantly changed and adjusted* your plans along the way. You have given it your best. You have to practice what you preach, and now here are a few scenarios that could play out over the course of your journey. In the first scenario all the things you've worked for came to fruition and all that could go right did go right. This will make up for the long hours, sleepless nights, tears and hardships. All of the days and sacrifices are paying off. You're enjoying the journey and you are operating in the zone.

In the second scenario, you may not be seeing your dreams pan out as expected. You're losing money and all your plans seem to be falling apart. You don't know whether to forge forward or to give up and concede to defeat. You may feel guilty because others have a stake in your success. You might have investors, family or even your reputation on the line. This could be the one thing you really thought you were good at and it just didn't work.

The third scenario is a gray area. Things are not bad, but they're not good. It's not awful, but it's not spectacular either. The questions become when do you keep going, hang in a little longer or just hang it up?

I can best explain this sequence through what I call the *America sports fascination.* Americans are obsessed with sports, and we love our sports heroes. At some point the question is asked, when will they retire? Should they go out at the top of their profession when they still dominate their opponents physically and mentally, or should they stay and compete when their dominance is gone? That question has been asked of great athletes from all eras, including Jesse Owens, Sugar Ray Leonard, Jackie Joyner-Kersey, Jim Brown, Muhammad Ali, Kareem Adul-Jabbar, Carl Lewis, Michael Jordan, Wayne Gretsky, Jerry Rice and George Foreman. The argument could be made for all sides about what, when and why these great athletes should do what they do.

For instance, why did the National Football League's greatest football player of all time, Jim Brown, leave in the prime of his career? Some fans felt cheated, not able to see Jim Brown continue to dominate. What made the greatest boxer of all time, Muhammad Ali, hang around longer than most thought he should? What made Carl Lewis last through four Olympics and win more track and field gold medals than anyone in American history? Some proved that coming back was the right move, as when Michael Jordan retired from basketball to play baseball, returned to basketball after two years to win three additional championships, before retiring again after one of his best basketball games ever.

You always hear this argument of when to stay and when to leave being discussed in sports because athletes reach a natural point where their physical skills diminish, leaving them with that question. Do I leave on top, or do I go out kicking and screaming? Believe it or not, these are the same questions you have to answer when you're reaching for your dreams. Just like an athlete, you have a set of skills that allow you reach the set of objectives you're trying to accomplish. Maybe it's pursuing a management position with your company or buying some rental property for your investment portfolio. Maybe it's a relationship you will be pursuing. Whatever the endeavor, you ultimately have to make a decision whether to continue on course, make some changes or move on to something different.

What gets lost in this pursuit of making your dreams work is the fact that you are consuming the one resource that is irreplaceable- time. Although time can't be replaced, many of us devalue it. We all live with the same 24 hours in a day and 7 days in a week. But some people are able to live more exciting and fulfilling lives in a month than others can live in a year, or even a lifetime. We seem to think God has given us an infinity of this precious commodity, so we tend to misuse it, misjudge it and even take it for granted. During the time management portion of my workshops, I do an exercise that allows participants to state what they would want most if they could change anything. The one answer participants request is a chance to live life over again. They would use time better, while making up for all the mistakes.

Again there are 1440 minutes in a day, 7 days in a week, 52 weeks in a year, and 900 months in a seventy-five-year lifetime.

By managing your goals, you can take advantage of the time given to you. This allows you to see and understand the big picture. Logically, you know that time passes, and once it's gone you can never get it back. Now answer honestly how important is your time and implementing your resources properly in the pursuit of your dreams? And what is the best thing you should be doing at any given moment with that time? Time plays an essential part of overall success, and being timely is an ingredient in your success.

You have heard of people or products that were born before their time. And because of this, their successes were not deemed relevant at the time. For instance, a major company made the fax machine years before there was a need. But once the overnight package carriers became popular, people wanted to get their documents even faster, making the fax machine an important resource.

Being timely deals with being in the right place at the right time with the right product or service for others to utilize. My definition for timely is "when your product is precisely what's needed and people are ready to take advantage of its services." Measurable results are the key words in whether your timing is right, because you can be busy doing the wrong things at the wrong time.

By asking yourself what is the purpose and projected outcome of your energy expended, you'll know whether you are on target to use your time properly. For instance, I'm typing this book at this time for the future result I'll experience knowing that you are reading it now. I'm spending my time wisely now in order to get a positive result later.

- Time is irreplaceable
- Some products are made before their time

Change and stress management

A question that needs to be answered is how do you know when to go forward or pull back? Life problems have a way of presenting the day-to-day task up-front and constantly in your face. You can easily spend your day handling crises or putting out fires. This in itself brings more attention to your day-to-day crises, while allowing the important projects to fall into the background, with lack of proper attention. Each and every day seems to be full of stress, movement and long hours. But when you look back and examine the time, you won't have much to show for it. Remember, there are millions of people working jobs and making a living every day. But very few of them are doing what they feel most passionate about. They failed to see their big picture, which brought about unhappiness and dissatisfaction. Their dreams seem to have floated off in the distance, never being within reach.

In answering the question of going forward or pulling back, I believe time management skills are a must. I equate it to the way I view the stock market. If you are going to invest, you go in with the idea of making a return on your investment. It would be fair to say that the long-term result you want to acquire is on the favorable side. But by the fact that you are investing, you know ahead of time that you are taking a risk. So before you start, you allocate and prioritize an acceptable amount of money that you can possibly afford to lose. You don't risk the rent money! Once you have exhausted that limit, the game is over. So your strategy is to prioritize a plan before you get emotionally involved. Set the parameters and work the plan as designed. Look at the investments over a set period of time. Then minimize the losses and maximize the gains, knowing that sometimes you have to take your losses and move on.

The same is true in life-you have to set the limit of acceptable loss. Then minimize your losses and maximize your gains. This is true for all successful people because they have the ability to see their goals or gains over a long period of time. But they have even an greater ability to know when they have hit that amount of *acceptable loss* and it's just not worth it, so they move on to the next thing. It's said that the average millionaire businessperson tried 23 different things before finding the thing that gave them their ultimate success. So you have to develop the plan and criteria to your time management. You have to know when to hold them and know when to fold them.

Thomas Edison tried thousands of inventions before he had success with the light bulb. How did he know how to manage his time between projects and which things to continue and which things to quit? By being *proactively obsessed for the moment*, he was able to give the things he was working on all of his attention at that time to see if it could work or not. This is an acquired skill, to focus intensely on the project at hand. There are people now who think that dabbling with something will bring success. What will bring success is a total commitment to that development. By dabbling in five or six ventures, you'll only find yourself wondering why nothing is working. Dabbling is more of a mindset that says, "I'm not pursuing the outcome to the best of my ability." It doesn't mean you shouldn't work on several things simultaneously.

On the other hand, some people stay with things far too long. For instance, perhaps a bad relationship should have ended five years earlier, but because the person kept going back, it never ended. You may have a job that you should quit but can't, or old toxic friends, even old items you can't part with.

In my workshops, I've worked with people who knew their company was downsizing and phasing them out. Even with the advance notice, they refused to look for a new job. One person had to be escorted out by security because they wouldn't leave their desk. What causes some people to react instead of proactively searching for a better situation? It could be their lack of a good time management system or their inability to measure the end results.

Practice Points:
- Be proactively obsessed for the moment
- Learn to minimize your losses and maximize your gains
- What will bring success on a project is a total commitment to it

"By studying something, you can become an expert in it. But by practicing something, you can become a master of it."

-E.J. "Edge" Bassette-

Reinvent yourself

My life, like yours, has been full of all emotions-of great joy to the piercing pain of losing loved ones to death, drugs or indifference. I have struggled to stay on course while experiencing both, great successes and tremendous setbacks. Both have given me the *reference points* to get back on track and handle situations differently, expecting different results. People have always asked me how I came out of the Chicago housing projects to become a high school and college football player, college graduate, top-producing salesman for two Fortune 500 companies, sales trainer, father, husband, business consultant, author, publisher, speaker and success coach.

Practice What You Preach

I'm quick to share with them the *character moments* that challenged me to *constantly change and adjust* my circumstances so that life could head in the direction I wanted it to, not the way it existed. I explain that because I wasn't able to have some things earlier, that fueled me to dedicate more energy to my positive efforts.

For instance, I think of the fear I had of living in the projects, especially during my high school years. The emotional setback I experienced when Mom and Dad divorced, and the lack of contact with her for twelve years. Missing most of the football season, my junior year of high school because of an injury was devastating. Not making the high school all-star football team my senior year, not earning a scholarship to college, and not making it to the NFL. Losing friends and family to illness, drugs and violence. Then in corporate America being denied opportunities to become a national sales trainer and manager for both of my previous employers.[12] Being turned down to lecture by numerous potential clients. All of these obstacles were the most important focuses of my life at that time. They all affected me negatively. Reinventing myself, allowed me a chance to change direction by going over, around, under or through the obstacle I was facing.

Think about what in your life you viewed as a major disappointment or setback that you were able to overcome.

1._____
2._____
3._____

_____

[12] Read "Silent Cry", by E.J. Bassette

Preach Points:
- We all struggle to stay on course
- Allow yourself a chance to reinvent yourself

What do you really want to do?

People don't just struggle when there are difficult times. There are many situations where people struggle with good opportunities. With opportunity comes responsibility. And everybody is not willing to step up to the plate to take on more responsibility. In the workforce, many people go to their jobs doing just enough work not to get fired. They hide from their boss hoping he or she will just leave them alone. The same thing happens in their lives. They hide out from life, hoping nobody ask them for anything. Before they know it, their lives are up.

In my trainings, I constantly try to get people to understand that the more you do, the more you're required to do. I have an exercise that poses two scenarios. The first is a person getting a promotion and more responsibility and the second is a person being fired. I have had more people wanting to get fired than promoted. They cite that the firing would free them up to do what they always wanted to do. The promotion would simply keep them locked into the job and lifestyle they don't really desire.

Stop and ask yourself the same question.

What would I do if I were fired today?
1. _____.
2. _____.
What would I do if I were promoted today?
1. _____.
2. _____.

Life after reaching your initial goal

There are times when everything goes right. You've accomplished what you set out to do, but still there is a big letdown. You occasionally hear of Olympic stars who practiced all their lives to reach the ultimate goal of participating in the Olympics and winning a medal. They had their goals, dreams and timetables in place, and through hard work, they accomplished their goal. But after they reached their height, one problem continued to surface: The ability to move beyond this phase of life. By not looking beyond their goals while still trying to exceed them, they were not able to apply more balance in their life, exposing them to new areas in which to accomplish.

This problem of not planning for life after winning can be just as devastating as losing. Losing can give you the hunger to try again and make it to the top. But winning makes some people lose the hunger, leaving them unmotivated and even depressed.

I had such an experience when I won my first major sales trip to Hawaii. That entire year I practically ate and slept sales in order to build the intensity, focus and dedication needed to accomplish this once in a lifetime feat. I was able to reach that dream of sharing the trip and joy with Donna in beautiful Maui. The disappointment started when the plane landed back in Chicago. The idea of going back to work was as devastating to me as a kid going back to school after a long, enjoyable summer vacation.

We can all set ourselves up for disappointments if we focus too much on the goal at hand without planning for life afterward. Having a plan B and a plan C keeps the mind working on subsequent goals that allows you an opportunity to flow right into the next phase or chapter in your life, even if major success or failure was the chapter you're closing. With the plan to move on, there is a more likely chance you'll continue without a major glitch.

- Have a plan B
- Look at what you accomplish as one positive experience of many to come
- Look forward to the next challenge in life

You are not responsible for your heritage, but you are responsible for your destiny

Understanding that life is for you to live to the fullest potential gives you an opportunity to take advantage of the choices you make. Life is ultimately about the choices you make that net the results you accomplish, whether it's walking a spiritual journey that increases awareness of the Creator in your life, and taking that faith and dedication to do something uniquely special on this planet, or just being the best parent in the world. You have been put in the driver's seat to consciously affect the outcome of your life. Don't settle for the limitations and low expectations set upon you by society, your family or your culture or ethnic background. Remember the earlier quote: "If you think you are or if you think you are not, you are right." It's your choice to believe.

By starting today you can change your conscious attitude about what you want to contribute to God, the world and yourself, and nothing will be able to stop you. One of the most disturbing signs that people wear is the label, "It can't be done." This world is full of people who are born into a situation where limitations were set before they were born. It takes those individuals to see that the chain has been placed on their brain and heart. That chain is an emotional, psychological chain that can be broken, giving them a limitless future.

One man who broke that mental chain was Nelson Mendela of South Africa. He spent 27 years in prison because he didn't believe in the physical and emotional bondage called "apartheid." His belief spurred a nation of people to have the

221

same conviction, eventually leading to his release from prison and rise to the highest office of the land, president of South Africa.

Other revered and loved figures are remembered and admired for their work even though they all could have held themselves back by the limitations of their color, religion or heritage.

President John F. Kennedy lived only 45 years, but was able to accomplish immeasurable amounts of good, despite others believing, somehow, that his religious background would be an obstacle. Dr. Martin Luther King, the great civil rights activist, lived only 39 years, but was able to reshape the destiny of a country with his dreams and aspirations. Malcolm X, the Muslim leader, managed in his 39 years to go from prison to become one of the most eloquent and effective advocates for poor people who were left out of the mainstream of America's success.

These three people and many others are revered in our minds for greatness in the results they accomplished and the way they served humankind despite the obvious limitations that were set on them. Each decided to look past the obvious and do it their way, refusing to let others dim their dream or hope for a better future. Even though none of them had a chance to see the end result of their vision, they left their marks on millions of others who crossed over to a better way of life because of them.

How did they do it? The answer is they believed in themselves. They didn't allow the limitations that others saw deter them. They got involved and pulled others with them. They didn't sit on the sideline and wait for someone else to quarterback the game. They saw a need and stepped in where there was a void. As you continue from this day forward, ask God to continue to give you the capacity to love and learn, and not to be afraid of giving to others or yourself.

Practice Points:
- Life is to live to its fullest potential
- Limitations are made to be broken
- Believe in yourself more than others believe in your limitations

"We need the ability to ask the right questions-no matter how tough- and then the patience to articulate the answers to those questions."
- E.J. "Edge" Bassette-

I can make more money, but I'll never feel better about what I do

Part of moving on to the next level comes when you feel you have accomplished everything you can at a certain level or point in your life. God has blessed me with an ability to assist others by sharing information in an informative, fun, exciting way to help them empower and change their lives. I have also been blessed to reach people of all walks of life and communities.

My personal life story has taken me from the projects of the inner city to a college degree, to corporate America, to the Fortune 500 companies, to becoming a founder of a speaking, coaching, professional and personal development company. I've been blessed to share my message through books, tapes, other products, speeches, training, scholarships and charity by giving time to those causes I felt needed my attention. My skills and passion are in teaching professional sales skills and personal development skills to those who are in need of bettering their lives personally and professionally. I started speaking full-time in the neighborhoods that needed attention.

That meant going into the heart of the inner-city communities, by way of schools, community centers and any other program that could get me involved.

By sharing vital life-saving information and skills with youth, I was able to give them alternatives and approaches that could bring success and happiness in their life.

Earlier in my speaking career, a school or community agency could never pay me my true worth, so I would make less money. And I knew that my sales, coaching and development skills developed over the decade in corporate America would be much more lucrative.

But, I had to do what my soul desired and needed to bring me closer to my beliefs. I needed to go back and make a difference. It's no different than any other person who has a mission that involves helping those less fortunate than him or herself.

In the past, I've even had other speakers, who were simply chasing financial rewards, laugh at my desire to make a difference. Just like my manager in the corporate world, some speakers said I needed to be a social worker, not a business speaker, consultant and coach. They didn't understand the larger vision. Professionally speaking to young people, especially in the inner city schools, positioned me to give more than I thought I had, but now I'm able to speak to any group anywhere. I also got a better feeling about who I was and what I was doing.

Those experiences gave me the same mental toughness and assuredness I had from growing up on the tough South Side of Chicago. I learned to go back into the neighborhoods on the West and South Sides of Chicago and look those young people in the eye and listen to their dreams and desires while instilling hope.

Over the years principals, and teachers would tell me time and again that they had never seen someone come in their school and have hundreds of kids hanging on to a person's every word. In many instances, teachers would tell me the children were incapable of sitting still and listening. But each and every time, those kids proved them wrong with their motivation and appreciation. This holds true for the suburban kids also. I've enjoyed all the thousands of young people, as much as they appreciated me. I would invite teachers to take advantage of my time and skills while I was available to teach in their communities.

Over the last few years, I've broadened my audiences to personal and professional training, professional one-on-one coaching with corporate executives, sales training and keynotes for adults. The organizations I've worked with include corporations, associations, chambers of commerce and business professionals.

A few years ago, I did three speaking engagements in one day: a school, a professional association and a corporation. I knew it was a blessing to be able to speak in all three of these environments. All three went very well. I received three standing ovations. God showed me that my uniqueness is truly my greatness.

You are truly unstoppable when you're doing the work you were chosen to do. Others will see the results and wonder how you were able to achieve what you achieve on such a high level. I have experiences like that all the time. For instance, a few years ago the Chicago Housing Authority came up with the idea to have a city-wide youth conference. This conference comprised of 700 young people from the ages of seven to seventeen years old, bringing them all together under one roof and holding self-improvement and violence prevention seminars. C.H.A. chose spring break for the event because of the potential violence that occurs when schools close, leaving hundreds of thousands of young people with nothing to do.

Using this time productively could expose the kids to new methods of thinking, and potentially save lives at the same time. It was an innovative and refreshing idea that had worked in New York. On the other hand, because it had never been tried in Chicago, the planners knew it had the potential to backfire. Because all of the kids were from different areas, they had different gang territories, which could lead to potential bad blood. That concern prompted a search to bring in the best speakers who could reach and relate to their experiences, and bring them up to a higher level of consciousness. So the coordinator, Gil Walker, and members of his staff, including many others who were familiar with my work, decided to have me as the opening lunch keynote speaker and workshop presenter.

The entire three-day conference was a complete success. The kids were wonderful each day, in spite of some adversity on the second day of the event. One of the coordinators said that there was gunfire in their neighborhood before her kids got on their bus. She was glad to have her kids out of the neighborhood and in and safe environment. I felt proud to be a person whom they related to as they rushed to the stage to ask if they could read my first book. At the end of the conference, the coordinators raffled off *Silent Cry* books and t-shirts. We also gave each kid a *Silent Cry* bookmark, which outlines the 10 success keys to stopping the violence.

Some people say these kids don't want to read, but I experienced with them and thousands of others the exact opposite reaction. I've been involved with the good in white kids, blacks kids and everyone in between, because they all want to read about things they are interested in. As a matter of fact, if all the kids I spoke in front of could buy my book, I would have sold hundreds of thousands of them, because whenever I've gone to speak, they've surrounded me asking if can they read the book about my friends and me.

At the end of that C.H.A. conference, hundreds of young people hollered out of the buses to me. They shouted my name and how much they loved and appreciated me as their friend. The organizers looked on with amazement because that week these kids had been exposed to singers, rappers, magicians and many others, but it was the words that I spoke that captivated their hearts. As the buses pulled off, one of the organizers said, "They knew you cared about them."

During lunch everyday, I didn't eat with the adults; I ate with the kids. I talked to as many as I could about their dreams and goals. I did everything I could to show those 700 kids I wanted to help them improve their situations.

Robert Taylor Homes, Stateway Gardens, Ida B. Wells, Dearborn Homes, Wentworth Gardens, Cabrini Green, The Ickkes, Altgeld Gardens, Henry Horner Homes; the absolutely toughest neighborhoods in Chicago were represented. On the last day, three young ladies presented another speaker and me with a thank-you card. The card was old and dirty, but that made it all that much more special. I know they may have found that card somewhere and put our names on it, but it was the thought that counted. Those ladies shared with us the fact that they didn't have any money to buy a card but they were appreciative because they knew we cared.

Starting off almost six years ago, I could have gone straight to corporate speaking for the money. But I have become a better person and speaker because of the route I chose. It also makes it easier for me to progress in other areas because I've paid my dues. Complete your obligation with yourself; then once you move on, it becomes a natural progression.

Practice Point:
- Give time to those causes you feel need attention

"Success is never final; failure is never fatal. It's courage that counts."
-Unknown-

Courage to fight

You have to know when to hold them and when to fold them. There can be a number of situations where it's better to walk away than have a confrontation. Then there are others times when you have to put on the gloves and defend yourself for what you stand for. This holds true for all of you seeking the empowerment to better your lives. To win big, you have to play big; and you had better be tough, because if you're not, everybody else will walk all over you. I'm not saying you should walk around with a tough-person image and a frown on your face. No, I'm not saying that at all, because if you put it out there like that, expect to get it back. You can have the outward appearance of a dove and the inward attitude of a tiger.

Your greatest victory will come when you control your attitude and how you approach your difficulties. Don't be an expert of bad news, but look at life from the positive and proactive state instead of a negative or reactive state. To be totally proactive means you'll have to fight through some psychologically, emotionally or physically tough times in order to have your goals and dreams become reality. Sometimes, it'll be similar to drowning and having to save yourself.

I remember in high school, that I hated to get near the deep end of the school swimming pool because I didn't know how to swim. Because I was a football player and my coaches (Coach Torian & the late John Mette) were also my gym teachers, I figured I had it made and I didn't have to learn to swim. One day that all changed when the coaches decided it was time I learned my lesson and they pushed me into the deep end of the pool. For a split second, I started going under until I decided to kick my legs and feet. I made a conscious decision not to drown and to swim to shallow water. The same is true when you're deciding anything. You can sink or swim. It's your choice.

You want to pick your battles wisely. I believe that when you would lose more than you would gain, then it's time to let it go. Now you are the only one who can determine if you're losing on the deal. By practicing the ten principles you preach, you've given it all you've got; if there is nothing left, then move on. There are plenty of people who fight the wrong battles and wind up depleting their resources or driving themselves into financial or spiritual bankruptcy.

But when it's in your value system and you believe in it, no matter how bleak the circumstances, you'll hang in to see it through. I've witnessed the courage of people with the lowest socio-economic status fighting for what they believe in-regardless of the circumstances.

One of these circumstances occurred in Chicago when there were some notorious gang-war confrontations. The projects known as Robert Taylor Homes and the Stateway Gardens were the center of attention. These housing developments are known around the country because there are 20 city blocks of 16-story buildings lined side by side, housing thousands of low-income families. The Chicago newspapers reported that the average income in the area is less than $3,000 a year. In part because the buildings are so close to each other, they serve as breeding grounds for gang activity in the area. Second, some of the buildings could have a 50% vacancy rate, leaving boarded-up apartments easily accessible to predators who stalk innocent little girls and boys for recruitment and abuse.

To top everything off, a major gang war broke out in the area, leaving the neighborhood in fear of gunshots and violence. As the gunfire escalated, enrollment in surrounding schools dropped by more than 50%. This included elementary and high schools, because parents refused to send their children out in the dangerous streets. Paul Vallas, former Chief Executive Officer of Chicago Public Schools, implemented a system to help the parents get involved with the neighborhood and walk the children to school. A number of brave parents decided join in and fight back, as they went door to door and challenged other parents to walk their children to school. Vallas appointed Dr. Kim Muhammad-Earl to run the program, and she hired me as one of the primary consultants, along with one of the top consultants in the school system, Dr. George Smith. Together, we trained the parents for this program, which became highly successful.

The media became aware of the situation. All the major stations came to the sessions to tape the proactive approach the Chicago Public School system was taking to solving this massive problem.

As I spoke to the parents I couldn't help but feel the hopelessness they must have felt, being economically deprived and socially degraded in one of the poorest communities in the country. The one thing I couldn't measure was their courage to fight for what was right. This displayed itself after the end of the workshops, when one of the parents walked up to me and handed me a piece of paper entitled "The Cross Room." She said that she wanted to give me a gift and asked me to read it when I had time. When I got home, I unfolded the piece of paper and read it.

The Cross Room

The young man was at the end of his rope. Seeing no way out, he dropped to his knees in prayer. "Lord, I can't go on," he said, "I have too heavy a cross to bear." The Lord replied, "My son, if you can't bear its weight, just place your cross inside this room. Then, open that other door, and pick out any cross you wish."

The man was filled with relief. "Thank you. Lord," he sighed, and did just as he was told. Upon entering the other door, he saw many crosses, some so large the tops were not visible. Then, he spotted a tiny cross leaning against a far wall. "I'd like that one, Lord." he whispered. And the Lord replied, "My son, that is the cross you just brought in."

On the bottom of the paper, the lady wrote, "I have grown and learned from what you have taught me. I will never forget you." As I left the violence-torn neighborhood to head back to my comfortable home and lifestyle, I realized I didn't give them a gift. They gave one to me. She had every reason to give up, to not care, because of the condition of her community. But she never complained and didn't want to trade her cross in for someone else's; she wanted to accept responsibility for her own. She had the courage to fight for her children and what she believed.

I received a valuable gift that day. And that program implemented in the school system has gone on to be a huge success in that neighborhood and others throughout the city. The City of Chicago has decided to demolish the high-rise housing developments. The residents are presently being relocated to other communities.

Preach Points:
- What do you do when you lose the battles?
- You keep fighting back until you win the war

God bless the child that has his own

In the hundreds of corporate and professional workshops I've conducted, I always ask the participants a question of who really wants to be working the job they have or doing the things they are involved in at that particular point in life. When this question is presented to the audience, sometimes as many as 90% of them wish they were doing something different in their careers and in their lives. The majority say they would do the things that are most passionate to them, which includes giving back to others. There always seems to be an overwhelming feeling to own something, whether it is a business or not-for-profit organization.

I suggest you go through the same thought process and figure the pros and cons of setting in place your life's ultimate design. Remember, you'll have different reasons for different things. Going into business for yourself could offer financial freedom or the business freedom to sell or own a dream. Or, it may offer you more flexibility to spend more time with family and friends. I know for a fact that having your own life, designed to your specifications will allow you a better opportunity for:

- Being your own boss: This gives you the authority to make the decisions over your time, business and family.
- Financial independence: You can develop a plan that allows you to only have the sky as the limit. Earning is only what you want it to be.
- Options for you family: You can have the flexibility of working from home, spending valuable evenings with your family.

Preach Points:
- The majority of people wish they were doing something different
- Go through the process of designing your ultimate life

Donna takes the challenge

While encouraging our children to actively read books, Donna would constantly look for books at the libraries and bookstores that challenged our children to read but would be informative, fun and educational about African-American history and how it was tied to our rich African legacy, pride and roots. As she looked from store to store she found herself disappointed with the lack of information available. Donna didn't want books that read like dry history books, but she was interested in the educational content and factual information those books contained.

One day, she and the kids came home again complaining about the lack of books available. So I stopped Donna in mid-sentence and said if you can't find the books you're looking for, why don't you write them yourself?

Donna has taken me up on the challenge. She is finishing her first book about some kids taking a magical trip to Egypt.[13] The book will be released this year. I will publish her book and make it available to schools and parents all over the country. This book is the first of a series that Donna will write. I'm proud of her because she saw a challenge and became the solution.

One in a Million

You have to be able to separate yourself from the pack and do the things that you believe are right. Too many people are living their lives solely for the approval of someone else. When others are controlling your destiny, you blow in the wind watching and waiting for direction. All you really need to know is that your principles and values are in line with the Creator. Thus, your mission is not to hurt, offend or mistreat anyone in the process of living out your dreams.

You must also understand that if you seek anything of value, others might attack you because of their fear or lack of understanding. Whenever you make a stand, someone will have an opinion that's different. This in itself shouldn't stop you from doing the things you believe are morally, spiritually and financially right for you and your loved ones. The only way to never upset another person is not to try anything, say anything or be anything, so why even exist?

People are asked to constantly choose or defend what they believe or whom are they aligned with about a variety of subjects. Most of the time the public is not fully aware of the whole truth, so their opinion can sometimes be based on limited or inaccurate information.

I learned this of the march in 1995, when a call for a million

---

[13] See our website at www.3Binc.com for more information

Practice What You Preach

African American men to go to the nation's capital for solidarity. Anybody who is familiar with the history of African Americans in America can sense that black men as a whole needed direction and focus. But that didn't stop the debates, and sometime downright anger displayed in many sectors of this country, as to why this march shouldn't take place.

The fact is that a Christian minister in the Chicago area had a vision of this massive gathering as a day of atonement. The Minister shared that plan with me a few years earlier than the actual Million Man March took place. He then shared his vision with his friends, and they decided to turn it into reality.

So when I heard about the date of the Million Man March, I called some friends and invited them to stand up and be counted by attending. A few of my close friends committed to show solidarity and wanted to make the trip to Washington, D.C. We didn't let factors like procrastination and fear become legitimate reasons for not participating and supporting the concept.

Being on the nation's capital mall that October 16th, 1995, was one of the most moving, positive experiences I could have ever been involved with. Being there with my big brother, Eddie, and good friends Tookie Tompkins and his Dad Percy Sr., Armand Mc Carroll and Tony Zeringue was wonderful. I felt a sense of pride as I looked around to see this mass of oneness in a million-plus faces around me. I couldn't help but think about the men who couldn't be there because of prison, probation restraints or financial concerns.

I claimed the Million Man March as my own that day by shaking the hands and hugging hundreds of black men from around the country. We all knew as African American men that we had to overcome the fear we had of each other and our failure to work together as a community to solve our own problems. We looked each other in the eyes as if to say, I'm sorry for the wrongs in our community and what we have done to our wives, mothers and children.

234

The Million Man March was a huge success. It was the largest gathering ever assembled in the history of this country. There were no disturbances or arrests; it turned out to be one of the most peaceful and well-organized events ever held.

The message of the Million Man March didn't stop that day. The promise was to come home and live that day for the rest of our lives. I've tried to live my life as a role model to my children, a leader in the community, and to live by the principles I've talked about in this book. I will never forget : I stood up as one in a million and took my place in history.

Preach Points:

- Separate yourself from the pack
- Whenever you seek something of value, you'll be attacked
- Stand up and be counted

"He who has done his best for his own time has lived for all times"
-Johann Von Schiller-

How do you become a part of history?

One way that time will record your journey on this earth is through your contributions to humankind. I believe becoming a part of history is a conscious choice, not an unconscious event. Most of us think so little of ourselves, we don't believe we have what it takes to have others remember us for the contributions we've made. We go through life not living up to any of our conscious expectations, while living vicariously through others who are revered and respected for their works.

Stop right now and ask yourself, "Am I going to do something worthwhile and significant?" You have what it takes. You don't have to live a life unfulfilled or of quiet desperation.

Some years ago, I made a conscious choice to become a person whom others saw value in. I asked myself this question: "What do great people have that reinforces their philosophy, commitment and contributions? The answer was books. They all have books they've written or had written about them. That single question made me think that I wanted to be in history and remembered for my contributions.

A few years ago, a lady called my office and said she had been in the library looking for the *Autobiography of Malcolm X*. As her eyes scanned the bookshelf, she noticed Alex Haley's acclaimed autobiography, *Roots*, one of this country's greatest stories ever told. She said excitedly, "Your autobiography, *Silent Cry*, sat between these two great American heroes. Congratulations for being in the library," she exclaimed. "That's a great accomplishment for you, being such a young man." Then she paused as though in deep thought, "Do you know that you are in history forever?"

I paused for a moment and said, "Yes , I planned it that way." What is the history you'll create for your children and their children to enjoy?

Preach Points:
- History is your contribution to mankind
- Becoming a part of history is a conscious choice

"Yesterday will soon be as far away as today.
Yesterday will turn into tomorrow. Your tomorrow
will remind you how you lived your yesterday."
-Kimberly E. Clark –sixteen years old-[14]

---

[14] Kimberly E. Clark, Author of "From my Thoughts to Your Heart, The Life of A Teen" Poetry- published by E.J. Bassette/check our website for order information

How to leave a legacy

The greatest way to become part of history is to leave a great legacy. That happens when you leave a gift, heritage or namesake. By using all ten principles of practicing what you preach, you give yourself an excellent foundation for a great legacy. You and I are nothing more than links in a chain through time that connects the past with the future.

We have been given the key to pass down to future generations. That key unlocks prosperity, success, happiness, pride, honesty, character and community. You have the key to all the questions, and most of the answers. Don't bury it under ignorance or lack of belief. Know that you have the key for future generations to use.

Imagine for a moment that your great-great-grandmother had a Bible she left you, dating back 200 years. And in this Bible she left a letter with your name on it. The letter says one of these two things in it. One version says, "This letter was written to you. I wanted you to know I lived, knowing one day you would be born. Even though I lived through some of the worst experiences of human history, I want you to know my thoughts and prayers were that I endure this pain so that one day you would be born to have a better life. Take this knowledge and propel yourself to unlimited greatness." How would you feel after you read that letter from your great-great-grandmother?

Now instead of the first version, let's say you received a different version. "I wanted you to have this letter because I wanted you to know how unhappy I am. I hate myself and thus hate you. I can't endure the sorrow and pain of these miserable days of existence. I wish I were never born, thus causing you never to be born."

Which letter would you want to get from your loved one-
the first or the second? Which one would propel you on to
greatness, and which one could leave you in hopeless despair?

Today you have a chance to leave a letter for the children
you love and the grandchildren you've never met. Yes, one day
you'll be part of that same history that your great-great-
grandmother was for you. What will you write and what
courage will you share as a witness of the turn of a new century
and new millennium? Will you hinder, discourage, and impede,
or will you empower, inspire, inform and teach. It will be up to
you.

Take a moment and write down your answer.

What are three ways your life's work will inspire
generations not yet born?

1._____
2._____
3._____

Preach Points:
- You have the key to all the questions, and most of the answers
- Which one would propel you on to greatness, and which one could leave you in hopeless despair?

Thank you for the opportunity to take you on this journey
over "The Edge."

You have what it takes. Continue to find in your heart the
capacity to give, share and love.

God Bless You

Recommended Reading
For you continued development

Highly recommended are the books of the authors who wrote *advance praises* in the front of this book. I highly encourage you to review that list. I recommend each of their books and additional growth tools for your development. I thank each of them for taking the time to support my book and efforts with their outstanding comments.

Other books recommended include:

E-Myth(Business), Michael Gerber

The Warren Buffet Way(Investment Strategies), Robert Hagstrom

Who Moved My Cheese(Change), Spencer Johnson, M.D.

It's Not Over Until You Win(Motivation), Les Brown

What Makes The Great Great (Life Skills), Dennis Kimbro

How To Win Friends and Influence People(Networking), Dale Carnegie

Awaken The Giant Within(Success), Anthony Robbins

7 Habits of Highly Effective People(Success), Stephen Covey

Pushing The Envelope(Management), Harvey Mackay

You Can Make It Happen(Success), Stedman Graham

The Millionaire Next Door(Business, Investment),Thomas J. Stanley Ph.D. & William Danko, Ph.D.

Order Form

Send to 3B Motivation, Training &
Development
P.O. Box 214
Matteson, IL 60443
(708) 747-6822
*Website: www.3Binc.Com
*Email:Edge@3Binc.com

Name _____

Business _____

Address _____

City _____ State _____ Zip _____

3B Growth Tools & Products

DESCRIPTION	QTY	COST
Two Motivational Cassettes -$20.00	_____	_____
Book/Practice What you Preach-$23.00	_____	_____
Book/Silent Cry-$21.95	_____	_____
Book/Magical Adventures in Ancient Egypt-(N/A) go to website	_____	_____
T-Shirts-$18.00	_____	_____
Bookmarks-$2.00	_____	_____
	_____	_____

Subtotal $_____

IL residents add 7.75%   *tax* $_____

Shipping & *Handling*   *$3.50 Per Item*

Total $_____

** Bulk orders & additional items are available. For more details, visit our website:**www.3Binc.com***

Method of Payment

Enclosed   **Check**_____ **Money Order** _____

Charge my Visa ____ **Charge my MasterCard** _____

Acct. # _____ **Exp. Date** _____

Signature _____

Please allow 4-6 weeks for delivery

E.J. "Edge" Bassette
Lead Consultant
Speaker/Trainer / Author

E. J. "Edge" Bassette's corporate experiences over 16 years has made him one of the country's leading consultants that speaks in the areas of sales, strategic personal and professional development.

As a lead consultant, Edge has created programs to assist companies, associations and other institutions to strategically achieve their goals by proactively taking responsibility for their own success. This approach maximizes the growth of the entire organization.

E.J. has trained in over 700 companies, associations, schools and other professional organizations reaching 200,000 participants.

Speaking-Training-Coaching-Books-Tapes

Let "The Edge" Help You Lead The Way!